A Dog For All Seasons

How to keep your dog happy and healthy throughout the year

Pennie Clayton

Copyright © 2023 Pennie Clayton

No part of this book may be used or reproduced without written permission

All rights reserved.

ISBN: 9798388244086

FOREWORD

Having known Pennie for many years I'm thrilled that she's finally put this book, A Dog For All Seasons, together, it's a book that is about dogs and for dogs, Pennie is a great advocate for properly understanding dogs both inside and out.

Understanding what dogs need on a daily basis, weekly basis, monthly and annual basis is vital, addressing their needs at all stages of life and constantly observing them to better address their comfort and wellness.

Pennie's insights and observations are the culmination of a huge amount of learning from courses, books, other professionals, experience and more importantly from the dogs in her life, her own dogs and those of her friends and clients. Too often people say how much they love dogs but do the dogs feel that love, we need to learn and constantly be aware of what love truly is; understanding of their innate needs, understanding their body language, movement, social skills, natural behaviours and this book covers it all.

Pennie's easy and common- sense approach makes this book a most enjoyable read and more importantly a book that your dog will benefit from. There are no commands or demands just simple advice on how to enable your dog to live their best life feeling safe, understood and appropriately loved in a way they enjoy.

It was an enormous pleasure and honour to be asked to write a forward for A Dog for All Seasons and I recommend everyone who purports to love dogs read it and share it. This book is refreshing and not about telling dogs what to do but teaches us what to do based on what our dogs are telling us. In short Pennie's book is fabulous.

Winkie Spiers

Member of APDT & ABTC

www.winkiespiers.com

A Dog For All Seasons

CONTENTS

Forward

Introduction

Acknowledgements

SPRING	1
SUMMER	28
AUTUMN	66
WINTER	104
ANY TIME OF YEAR	152
Appendix	168
Resources	173
References	174

INTRODUCTION

This book has been a labour of love!

There has not as far as I know been a book that addresses how the seasons affect our dogs and it is based on the many thoughts and articles I have written over the last few years.
Some of the posts originate from a group I run on Facebook called Enhancing the Life of Your Hound and some have been put together specifically for the book.

The subject matter is important because as we live beside our dogs and the years tick by it is easy to underestimate their needs and forget that we have the important job of observing and reacting to any problems our dogs may be having so we can ensure they are happy and healthy.
Enriching and improving our dogs' lives should be something that we all aim for although many of us underestimate just how important it is to continually ask whether we are providing the best lives for the dogs we live alongside.
This goes beyond beds, treats and visits to places that we believe our dogs enjoy. If we understand more about how our dogs experience the world this provides a lot of food for thought. Even if we understand basic specific needs, these needs constantly change and vary not only with the seasons but as they grow older which is why this book is divided into sections.
Every day is different and will often necessitate specific action to help ensure our dogs are comfortable

Although we don't have much control over the seasons, we can be prepared so we are able to help our dogs cope

during the changes that the seasons bring.
Some dogs will cope well in the cold and other dogs prefer the warmth of the spring and summer, and this should assist us to make good decisions on behalf of our dogs.

The format of this book differs to the "norm" as it has been written in segments so it can be read in any way the reader chooses.

If input is needed on how to cope with a firework phobic dog a plan can be found in the autumn section. or if your dog is behaving weirdly during Christmas you can look under the winter section
The book starts with the Spring and then continues on as the year progresses from summer into autumn and winter.

Some of the posts are not specific to any time of the year but they are often written in response to my own observations of my dogs as the seasons change and to things that have happened in my professional life.
This includes advice and information on therapies, pain and illness as well as the joyous side of our dogs' lives

Any mistakes found in this book are my own as I had trouble surrendering the manuscript to anyone, I have to admit to this being on of my many faults!

To make it easier for me to write the pronoun "he" has been used throughout the book

ACKNOWLEDGMENTS

I would like to thank Winkie Spiers for writing such a lovely foreword and also Laura Dobb of The Slow Dog Movement for her everlasting encouragement and support while I was putting this book together.

Also, to my many wonderful dogs that I have been privileged to have lived with especially my wonderful lurcher Flynt to whom I owe an enormous debt for teaching me so much
I also need to pay tribute to all of my wonderful greyhound girls, because my life has been enriched by their presence and their good humour.

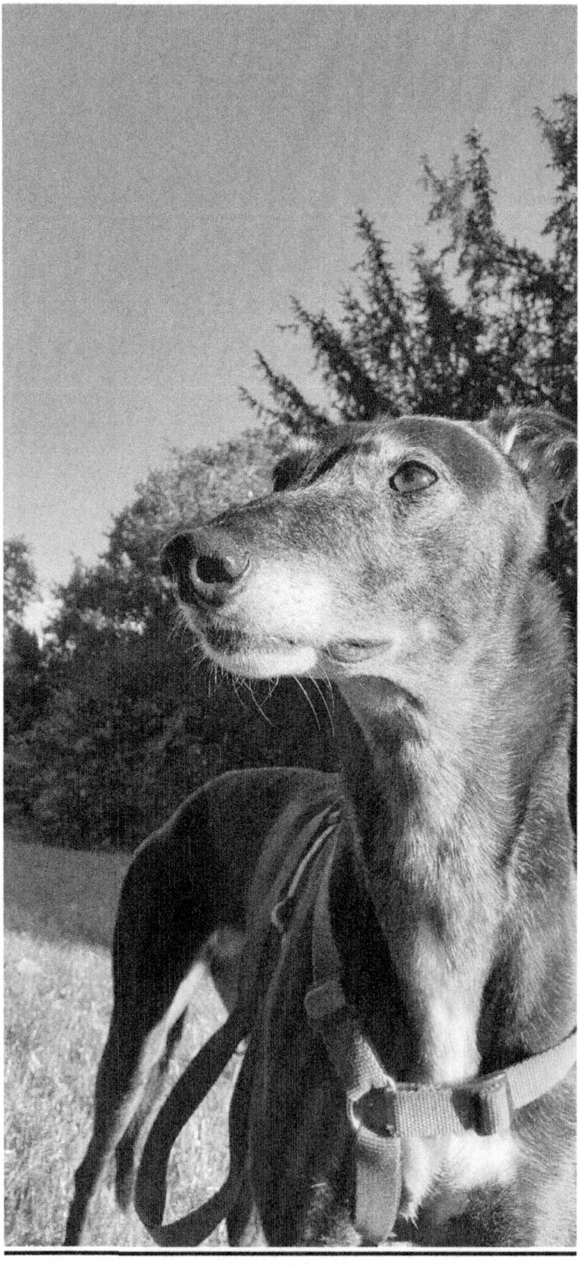

SPRING

The Spring is probably the best season for our dogs. The days are lengthening and becoming warmer. The dogs that dislike the dark and associate it with fireworks can begin to relax and there is little danger of heatstroke.

It is generally too early for thunder storms which can create worry and anxiety for many dogs and there are no major celebrations which impact on everyday life apart from Easter, but unlike Christmas, New Year and Halloween it is a very gentle celebration. The whole world slowly becomes green and mellow. There are more opportunities for leisurely walks and the light changes in quality from dusky damp to bright and inviting.

Spring is also synonymous with growth and new life so there a are a number of puppy segments included within this section

This chapter as with the entire book reflects not only on the Spring but looks at some issues that are current no matter the time of year it is.

"Dogs are our link to paradise. They don't know evil or jealousy or discontent. To sit with a dog on a hillside on a glorious afternoon is to be back in Eden, where doing nothing was not boring--it was peace."― Milan Kundera

Here comes the sun!

Sometimes the spring gives you whiplash, it can go from wet and windy to sunny and hot within a few hours in the UK.

A Dog For All Seasons

It is as well to be prepared in regards to our dogs because even during early spring temperatures can fluctuate without warning. While heatstroke is not really a huge concern at this time of year it is just as well to take precautions if you take a trip out with your dog in the car. If the sun is appearing look for a shady area to park under so if the heat increases while you walk, the interior temperature of the car won't exceed what is comfortable for your dog especially if the morning started off chilly, it takes time for dogs to acclimitise to increases in temperature so considerations of this nature are helpful. This is a good time to assemble a warm weather back pack which should include a towel, (which can be soaked with water if needed) and some surgical spirit.
If the heat does suddenly create a problem surgical spirit can be put onto the dog's pads and help bring temperature down rapidly.

This kind of pack should also include a cool coat, and a container of water. A spring backpack doesn't have to include fully- fledged summer kit, but rather one that has the warm weather essentials so that random periods of heat don't catch you out in early to late spring.

Hard ground

I work with horses as well as dogs. Horse people spend an inordinate chunk of the year worrying about hard ground and the effect it has on their horse's legs and feet. This preoccupation generally starts in early Spring as the ground dries out

But this issue is not solely confined to horses, few people give a thought as to the impact it can have on their dogs.
Hard ground does have the benefit of being "supportive"

in as much as dogs won't slip and slide as they might when walking through mud that sticks to feet and paws, and of course many dog owners are thankful that they don't have to wash mud off of their dog's bodies, legs and paws.

But, have you ever really thought about the effect hard ground has as a dog runs or jumps to catch balls if the surface is like rock? Running, turning sharply, taking off and landing on surfaces which are unyielding have a concussive effect on joints, and is extremely damaging, and has a culminative effect. Ground can also be pitted and uneven as it dries out too, which adds another dimension to the likelihood of injury and soreness within a dogs' body and can have an ongoing influence on joints as your dog ages. Concussion is rarely discussed in regard to dogs, and unlikely to be recognised as a contributory cause for lameness.

This is highlighted because prevention is better than cure- once arthritis raises its head it is too late. It is true that softer ground can create problems but it certainly never has the implications that hard ground does. Cases of arthritis are increasing in dogs. It has many causes but hard, and slippery surfaces have a leading role on the health of joints and overall physical health.

A certain amount of movement on hard ground is unavoidable but in order to provide our dogs with interesting walks we need to be seeking a variety of textures and surfaces. For instance, grassy and wooded areas provide a supportive layer of leaves/pine needles to absorb some of the effects of fast exercise, and if available beaches and sandy areas are good for joint health.

We do not need to be living in amazing areas to seek these areas out. Proprioception is a major sense and it needs stimulating regularly in order to maintain good balance and combines to create good connections between the body and brain.

Correct movement also stimulates the tactile and vestibular senses. This contributes to making our dogs lives richer and more varied.

Our routines *should* vary according to each season, so consider what is underneath your dog's feet, and the effect that concrete or rough surfaces may have on joint health. Being aware of these issues will stave off injuries and pain as dogs age.

You don't have to walk your dog *every day*.

There are many reasons to consider this statement. One of the most important reasons for acting on it is if a dog has been newly rehomed or if you have a reactive dog. Stressed dogs can suffer from being overstimulated and can become overwhelmed in a very short period of time.

We are all constantly being told that dogs need exercise. Certainly, we know that if a dog is overweight exercise should be part of weight reduction, but it is becoming common knowledge that it doesn't have as huge an impact on weight as was once believed.

If you have ever watched any documentaries on weight control which detail how many calories are lost during a workout, you may already be aware that weight loss is not significant during exercise. (But just in case this seems like an irresponsible statement, it is understood that exercise should most certainly be part of any weight control programme and has a huge positive impact on mental health)

But at this point we are discussing the problems experienced by dogs that are fearful, newly rehomed, or have suffered trauma, and the most important thing we can ever do is to help our dogs feel safe. Safety is a basic need and we can't help a reactive or easily hypervigilant dog by presenting him day after day with overwhelming situations.

Duvet days are essential for all dogs but in particular for those dogs that are experiencing extreme anxiety outside the home. Quiet days promote rest, sleep and recovery and help to restore wellbeing. Walks can be replaced with enrichment, but be careful not to demand too much or create frustration. I am a huge fan of enrichment, but it needs to be done with the dog in mind and it should not involve ever increasing challenges. Every dog has favourite pastimes and it is important to stay within this comfort zone.

Duvet days are not just for humans they are for dogs too!

Preparing for summer holidays with dogs

It is that perfect time of year when not only do the evenings and mornings become lighter and warmer, but it seems possible to at long last anticipate sunny days.

It is a perfect time to plan some days out with your dog as well as holidays. There are now numerous places to stay that accept and welcome dogs and some beautiful areas of the UK to choose from. Even so they are often expensive so camping remains a great option if you have dogs. It is easy to plan your days and there are less things to worry about like dog hair being shed over furnishings to and of course no restrictions on where dogs can sit and relax. If camping is not an option holiday homes certainly fill a void, but some do have rules about the number of dogs allowed, and where they can sleep, so do check before you book.

If you do decide to camp, you may need a few extra dog related items but the positives are more numerous than the downsides especially if you select an area which is dog friendly such as Norfolk or Suffolk. There are numerous beaches in Norfolk that are open to dogs all year round but they are particularly beautiful during the summer especially if you visit late in the evening or get up extra early. One of the perks of holidaying with your dogs is to share the moment as the sun rises especially if it is then followed by breakfast at a dog friendly café

Once upon a time, I shared a camping holiday with one of my greyhounds who spent hours outside the tent just watching everything going on around her until late into the night, she was so entranced she didn't seem to notice the time. Some pleasures are very simple and there is nothing better than being amongst nature with a dog.

A little tip- if you do holiday with your dog always fill a few bottles with water from your home to take with you- many dogs dislike the taste of unfamiliar water and the situation can quickly escalate and cause dehydration. If you gradually add the "new" water from your campsite or holiday home most dogs find the change more acceptable

Upbeat or downbeat?

Do you understand your dogs' general take on life? Obviously, many things can affect how their outlook on life such as pain, stiffness, discomfort and mental health problems.

An important consideration is to consider the rules we

impose on our dogs, because it has a bearing on happiness and contentment. Do the rules we insist on both contribute and enhance the lives of dogs or do they make them more difficult or even miserable?

Humans have a lot to answer for, and we have been conditioned to expect dogs to behave in specific ways but we do have to understand that many of the things we insist on can be difficult or even detrimental for our dogs. A dogs' needs are very different from our own in many respects but overall, it has to be said that they have a natural inclination towards positivity- so if a dog is downbeat, stop for a moment and question why this might be. We can affect state of mind in either direction. If we ask our dogs to do things which are neither necessary or of benefit to them this can very easily lead to depression and anxiety.

Is a specific behaviour or exercise that is constantly asked for really necessary? This might be something we have been insisting on every day of their lives, for example sitting before meals are given or not allowing a moment to pause at the door before stepping out for a walk- this in particular is relevant as many dogs like to stop for a heartbeat or two before stepping from the front door so they can sniff the air and pick up scents. Never forget that dogs use their noses in the same way as we use our vision.

If we examine why we ask for these behaviours, we may realise they are not necessary and by ceasing to impose them it will be benefit to our dogs but unlikely to create any problems for us.

It can only be a positive if their lives include fewer unnecessary rules. There is nothing better than watching a happy optimistic dog, and we do have the power to change their outlook. Our dogs deserve the kind of carefree lives that we would choose for ourselves.

Advocate for your dog and gift him with the life that he would choose for himself.

Movement and moving

Yesterday while I was walking one of my dogs, I did something to my knee, I have an old injury from many years ago which was a result of me breaking my leg. Old injuries never really disappear and need looking after, and this is no different for our dogs many of which have injuries that have never healed completely. The right kind of movement enables our dogs to focus on their balance and think about exactly how and where they place their feet.

To review-walk involves all four feet hitting the floor at separate times. "Correct trot " involves the dog using diagonal movement (one hind leg and the opposite front leg) but often due to compensation (pain related) or being restricted when walking -a dog may pace, which can be seen by the dog moving both feet on the same side of the body at the same time. Pacing is not desirable and the pure gaits of walk and trot are far preferable as they indicate good health and absence of compensation

It is good to recap on the movement because it involves so many of our senses. We are familiar with hearing, smell and vision but our senses work together in ways that we are not always conscious of. Make a habit of watching carefully as your dog moves. This doesn't mean you should curb your dogs' movement but do allow him to investigate and explore without interruption.

A dogs' focus will be on how to balance and navigate

the areas that are being traversed. These seemingly simple tasks co-ordinates the vestibular, visual and proprioceptive senses. If we only walk our dogs along flat paths they are likely to gradually lose the ability to adjust to what is underneath their feet.

Ageing is not a disease and dogs don't necessarily stiffen up as they age but this will happen unless we give them some choices as to where and how they exercise. Providing a portion of exercise which is voluntary and without restriction or coercion is really valuable. This is particularly relevant in the case of ex racing greyhounds, because many retire as a result of injury. Retirement is hastened by the fact that tracks are all left- handed, don't always have good surfaces and there may be a possibility of greyhounds suffering from hypermobile joints. Other breeds of dogs may share this problem too but they do not start with the disadvantages of the racing greyhounds.

The more details we have of an individual dog's history and the breed the easier it is to ensure good mobility is maintained. Providing the right exercise should not be formulaic but our wishes are often in opposition to what is needed by our dogs. Choice of how to move and when, of what to focus on and what to interact with on walks is important. It is understood that we might need to regulate some of this in order to keep our dogs safe but the studies of street dogs inform us that they are able to advocate for themselves

This is why correctly set up enrichment areas are so important. It is a huge benefit for a dog to have a few sessions a month where they have choice not only of where to explore but to fulfil natural behaviours. This should include stepping on and off objects, varying textures under their feet and how to position and their bodies around obstacles. All are are incredibly valuable to health and wellbeing

Dogs (and ourselves) also need good visual reference points to orient themselves which may be why so many newly rehomed dogs falter when they step out of the front door. If an area slopes directly ahead this can distort senses and create situations which dogs can find difficult to negotiate especially if they suffer with pain or sensory problems. This can lead to freezing and planting.

Our dogs often know best and if we present them with the same kinds of walks and the same types of terrain, we are doing them a disservice.

Does your dog have friends?

This question is aimed not at whether your dog has human friends or passing dog acquaintances you may meet in the park, what it asks is if your dog has dog friends that he hangs out with.

Dogs don't have as many friends as we might think and if we look at our own lives this is comparable, as we may have no more than 2 or 3 solid friends.

There is also another group that needs to be considered- puppies need friends too but they also need older dogs as mentors. If a young puppy does nothing other than play with dogs of his own age then the risk is that they become "play monsters". This leads to less than perfect social skills. Older dogs act as teachers, just as children learn from school teachers and other responsible adults that are around them. Play most definitely has a valuable place in a dog's life but not to the exclusion of learning valuable social skills from older accomplished dogs.

Returning to the idea of firm friends I once read that the definition of a really good friend was someone you could ask to help you if you needed to bury a body! No questions asked! I am not sure I would want to put any of my friends through that, but I do know they always appear when I need them. These are the kind of genuine friends that our dogs need. The bonds that form when they have a genuine connection are very secure and while there maybe the occasional dispute it fulfils the need for social contact with other dogs.

If our dogs don't have these firm friends, we need to search and provide them because being a social species means friendships are an important part of their ethogram.

That "hot bath moment"

This is a term often used by Dr Amber Baston regarding anxious and chronically stressed dogs. The thought behind the hot bath moment is to find something that dogs find truly pleasure-able but non exciting. For example, we humans might look forward to a hot bath, a cold beer, or a cup of tea while sitting outside in the sun after a long difficult day. Certainly, we all have our version of that moment when we let out a sigh of contentment as the worries seep away.

But what would a dogs' equivalent of that be? Examples should not include an inelastic need (such as sleep or food) because these should already be in place. In the case of my dogs, their hot bath moment is digging a hole, rolling in sand or taking a long and unhurried walk where they are given the choice of which direction to take and where they can pause to sniff when they desire. More attention should be paid to thinking about what our dogs truly enjoy-rather than what we *think* they enjoy.

A dog's day should not consist entirely of what we choose for them, neither should it consist of "yo- yoing" between fast activities and sleep, there must be room in the routines of our dogs that can be defined as sheer pleasure, and it should be the dogs' idea, most definitely not indicated or chosen by us.

Be more dog!

Unwell

We all know how upsetting it is to have a dog that is unwell. Often it is temporary due to unsuitable foods that have been ingested or other similar misadventures which dogs often get into. Some dogs can be a bit accident prone but the minor signs are easy to miss and we can be a bit dismissive of "off days". Ill health is inconvenient, both in ourselves and our dogs, it can upset plans cause arguments and is often open to debate when it comes to our dogs.

We can use any excuses we like but our dogs are generally upbeat and bouncy, this is why it instantly recognisable when changes occur. A dog that moves slower than normal, or consistently refuses food is very unlikely to be "acting up" or starting to become a "fussy eater". It is not in a dogs' nature to turn his nose up at food and this is one of the reasons why we have to take our responsibilities seriously when we live with a dog.

Recently people have been talking about dogs being particularly fussy and manipulating their carers into giving them a greater variety of foods so therefore "rewarded" for this picky behaviour. This is extremely unlikely. A dog needs sufficient choice and variety in the diet so it supplies all the necessary nutrients and vitamins needed. It is not a question of bad behaviour.

People with cancers have reactions to specific foods as they may associate them with times when they have had chemo and were particularly unwell. Our dogs are no less likely to suffer from taste aversion if there are negative associations with specific foods. This does not exactly belong under the heading of being unwell but these things should not be overlooked.

The signs of ill health are just as visible in our dogs as they are in ourselves but while *we* might be able to afford to ignore feeling nauseous or lethargic, we cannot afford to ignore these symptoms when it comes to our dogs. Dogs in particular are notorious for the ability to be stoic. It is quite likely to be one of the hangovers inherited in the evolution from wolf to dog. By the time a dog is showing symptoms of being unwell he may well be very sick.

Let's begin by looking at some signs. If you check the internet, you will find all the obvious suspects listed. However, we are discussing the slight fluctuations that happen before full- blown symptoms develop. Part of what all of our bodies do is to eliminate old and dying cells, this process is called apoptosis. This process eliminates potentially cancerous and virus infected cells and help to maintain balance in the body.

This is a small part of the body's very important purpose of keeping the body running smoothly. It may not seem related but something as simple as a change to a dogs drinking habits can begin to affect homeostasis. Water not only hydrates the body but eliminates toxins. A change is your dogs' drinking habits should always alert us to potential problems. Even though it would not be easy for a vet to pinpoint health problems through an observation of changes in the amount a dog is drinking it is most definitely worthy of being noted. This is why a simple daily diary is important. Even tiny fluctuations in normal daily activities should be jotted down and monitored as these will give advance warning of potential problems.

For example, people often worry when their dog eats grass. There are many reasons for this behaviour including how juicy and sweet spring grass is, this is because it contains sugars. Grass eating has also been shown to help our dogs become calmer, but it can also signal stomach upsets.

These are easy to pick up on as the stomach starts to gurgle and these sounds can vary from very quiet to loud. If you put your ear to your dogs' stomach you might hear a soft gurgle which is entirely normal, but a louder and more audible noise should be something you pay attention to especially if it occurs on a regular basis.

Apathy should also be on the list of seemingly subtle changes which need our immediate attention. A dog should not be quiet or disinterested. If this occurs in an older dog it should not be considered normal or just a part of getting older. It signals ill health. Dragging an unwilling dog out for a walk and dismissing it as "stubbornness" if he refuses to walk at a normal pace is a dangerous label to fix onto this behaviour. It is equally dangerous to overlook younger dogs and puppies if they are quiet. Puppies should be anything but quiet if they are healthy.

If this is combined with an event such as recently being put on medication, a bad fright, or a raided bin then this could constitute more than just a "quiet day". Lethargy is one of the symptoms that should alert us to the fact that all is not well. It is easy to dismiss, but a major health problem can often appear innocuous in the beginning

Unusual postures and frequent stretching also provide visible evidence of health problems. Knowing when your dog stretches during the day and *how* he stretches is important. For instance, constant and unusual stretches especially in "prayer position"- front legs stretched out with haunches pushed up can signal an internal blockage

Bad breath is another thread that is worth picking at. Dogs of all breeds can and do get bad teeth and decay does occur but bad breath does not always signal problems with teeth or within the mouth. Changes in the smell of breath are significant and it is worthwhile having a worm count done rather than just ordering worming tablets from the internet or supermarket. The companies that do worm counts give specific information about the presence of worms and which types are present in the gut. A specific and beneficial worming programme can then be put in place which will be of greater benefit than a general wormer.

Bad breath can also signal kidney disease and this can smell like ammonia, or if breath smells sweet like pear drops this can signal diabetes, exactly as it would in a human - a sweet foul musty smell can indicate liver disease. These problems will also be mirrored in urine and there will be significant changes in colour if a dog develops any of the conditions mentioned above.

This is a good place to discuss inflammation and why it is so necessary. The majority of people think of inflammation as a negative thing, but inflammation is a life saver and a necessary process when it comes to healing. If your dog is not feeling on form his body will already be responding via his immune system.

When infection is detected by the body it is already launching an all- out attack on bacteria and/ or viruses. The immune system initiates the process of sending white blood cells, antibodies and other mechanisms to the compromised area to rid the body of foreign invaders. This can then result in rashes, fever (heat inactivates many viruses) or malaise but this is the result of the body eliminating infection from the body. The body will also release interferon which blocks viruses from reproducing and antibodies will target any viral threat. Bacterial infections are dealt with is a similar way but toxins are rapidly produced and will prompt a massive immune reaction. This is unpleasant but it is visible proof that the immune system is fighting the threat. It is only if the inflammation becomes chronic rather than acute that we need to become really concerned. Any disease can be accompanied by emotional symptoms which is why it is always best to get your dog checked out even if no physical symptoms can be seen.

It is hard to prevent illness but our dogs' bodies operate under a similar system to our own. If we think carefully about exercise, reduce stress, provide good places for them to rest and sleep and supply our dogs with a good diet then there is a very good chance that we can avoid chronic illness.

If you sense that your dog is unwell, throw the social diary out of the window (just as you would for yourself) and give him some duvet days to rest and recover and monitor him carefully. Just like us many chronic illnesses can be avoided by taking time out.

Our dogs only have us to advocate for them so make sure the subtle signs of illness are not missed by the one person that can actually do something positive. That person is you.

Is my dog really in pain?

Despite the amount of information which is freely available many people are often in denial about pain issues that their dog is experiencing. We all have pain at some point in our lives and many people have to deal with it on a constant basis. It is depressing, disabling and inhibiting, and this is no different from our dogs. It *is* hard to believe that a dog has pain when he appears to be running around with the kind of vigour he has had since he was a puppy.

We humans like our social activities, and we very often bring a dog into our lives to compete in various canine disciplines.

But there is a cost. High energy activities tax our dogs mentally and physically. When dogs are running fast, performing leaps, catching balls, jumping and rushing to get around obstacles their joints, tendons, ligaments and muscles are working hard, and this can lead to damage.

It is a fact that more dogs suffer from arthritis than ever before, and the last known figure (in the UK) showed that 1.2 million dogs experience damage to joints which leads to arthritic changes. This means pain is present.

Adrenaline and cortisol have an influence on the brain and dogs are unlikely to register pain if these hormones are coursing through the body as they run, these chemicals are natural pain killers It is normal for the body to release these chemicals during fast activities, but what should be regarded as abnormal is a daily release of these chemicals as the result can be the body moving into a state of chronic stress. So, when the question is raised about whether a dog is in pain, there are many things to consider including our opinions about various competitive dog sports like agility and flyball.

Dogs often get addicted to chasing and running games. Their reaction to running, jumping, or a fast moving agility class or flyball can look to be one of joy. But observe carefully, because addiction can look a lot like enthusiasm, and pain is temporarily put on hold as the excitement builds. If a dog is completing agility courses, or doing many runs of flyball however fast this doesn't mean he is *not* in pain.

The symptoms of pain include (and this is not a complete list, many more exist)

- Unable to settle after exercise or competition
- Refusal to eat
- Finding it hard to get onto the sofa
- Unable to do a complete shake off along the entire body
- Uneven or unusual muscle development or atrophy of muscle, this is noticeable if the dog's collar needs to be let out as this indicates build up of muscle in the forehand to compensate for pain in the hind legs
- Allodynia-the definition is "pain due to a stimulus that would not normally provoke pain". An example might be a dog flinching and moving away when being touched

Many people are in denial and are not paying enough

attention to changes. They ignore the subtle signs and refuse to see a gradual deterioration

We must learn to look at behaviour change, because it always signals pain, discomfort or intense anxiety.

Socialisation (and the puppy connection)

Finding a quiet area to walk with your dog is one of the best investments in time. Not only is this of benefit for older dogs who dislike being jumped on by younger dogs, it is really important for puppies and adolescent dogs too. This might seem an unlikely thing to suggest, but areas of peace, quiet and shade are integral for dogs because just like us there are times when a dog doesn't want to be social!

Puppies in particular need care. There is *so* much recent research and evidence these days which explains why the old model of "socialisation" should be discarded. But, despite the hard evidence the old ways still prevail.
The brain of a puppy develops rapidly during the first few months of life. This coincides with being introduced into a new home.

Part of building social skills is watching things going on around us, how many times have you stopped to watch something? It might be something you have never seen, or it might be a familiar situation that is happening in a place that you weren't expecting it. Puppies like to do this too. As they watch, they process what is going on and it is stored in their memories. If we rush away from an unfamiliar situation a puppy is more likely to form negative associations than if he is allowed to watch. Young dogs need to process the world around them and we need to allow them to do this. Among the situations that a young puppy is expected to cope with is meeting people. But do this with care because we run the risk of making these situations negative and this results in "flooding".

Flooding is defined as an individual (or animal in this case) being exposed to a maximum anxiety producing situation or stimulus without any attempt to lessen or avoid anxiety. As far as socialisation is concerned this is very negative and can create mental discomfort. If many people stroke a dog or puppy when they try to move away we create an episode of flooding.

A young puppy is unable to express just how difficult this is and often results in the puppy jumping up. A puppy has little control over this reaction and this regularly leads to some kind of punishment. We reap what we sow, and a puppy that is uncomfortable in these kinds of situations is often ignored. To become better carers, we need to recognise that busy places with lots of people only create conflict.

Socialisation is a long game.

We do not have to complete it at a sprint. If we see it as something to be "completed" as fast as possible, it is likely that problems will occur as a puppy reaches adolescence. It takes a certain stubbornness on our part to go against the mood music, and instead of immersing a puppy into busy people rich situations the following should be included in everyday life experiences, but at weekly intervals. Little adventures can be fun. These might include short car rides to new places, visits to check the *outside* of the vet's surgery, brief visits to a good friend or a take a cup of coffee to visit places like the local churchyard where exploration can be encouraged. While on this subject select puppy classes with care, the less pressurised and more enjoyable the classes are the better.

Taking care does not cost us anything. If we provide gentle introductions, this empowers and helps puppies to build good solid social connections.

Sensory integration

Very soon, there will be dog shows and events starting to be advertised. Many of us love to attend dog shows and events that are filled with dogs. But, for a percentage of dogs these events are unbearable and their discomfort can go unrecognised There may be too much noise, too many novel scents and too many people. If an event is really busy dogs inevitably spend a lot of time trying to avoid other dogs and trying to cope with bumping up against people's legs. The general public rarely understand that not all dogs like being stroked or petted- yes, some dogs do enjoy the attention, but many don't.

I was listening to the radio this morning and there was an item about an upcoming event at the British Museum, so when I returned home, I looked it up. It turns out that this type of event is something that many museums run. The events are for children with autism and other similar conditions such as ADHD. Children with these conditions find it impossible to cope with the normal hurly burly that is part and parcel of being in busy public places. These special sessions are run during early weekend mornings, and give children time and space to explore without being compromised. The one that was featured at the British Museum included a quiet area where children could go if they needed a break.

There is current research that is investigating the possibility of whether dogs and other animals could be on the autistic spectrum. Those of us with dogs may already have a gut feeling about this question, and my opinion is that they do share many of the conditions that humans experience, but it just hasn't gained a lot of attention up until now.

Most certainly there are dogs that can't cope with busy environments and suffer from too much sensory stimulus and overload. Knowing this is a possibility it would be helpful if event organisers took note and altered stands and areas that sell food easier for dogs to navigate so that they are not constantly forced into close proximity with people and other dogs.

But an even better step would be for dog carers to think clearly before taking dogs to events. When planning your spring and summer activities do consider how your dog responds to hectic environments
. Not all dogs love busy places and if they appear to go a little bonkers, this does not necessarily mean they are having a good time, it may mean it is their version of hell.

Do you ever wonder why you see greyhounds wearing muzzles?

If you happen to be out and about with your dog and you see a greyhound wearing a muzzle, how should you react?

What needs to be explained is that greyhound rehoming centres always advise people to walk newly rehomed greyhounds with muzzles on. Muzzles do not mean that greyhounds are aggressive, or likely to bite or they are a threat.

A newly rehomed greyhound is trying to make sense of his new world. They have generally lived in a kennel environment since being born, have strict routines, spend their lives surrounded by other greyhounds and have rarely seen other breeds of dogs. More importantly if they have raced, they have been expected to chase a small fluffy contraption around a track from an early age.

Before being rehomed ex- racing greyhounds have never been to a beach, a large park, or a place where dogs run off lead. They will not have seen squirrels chasing around the trees and the sensory overload is *huge*. So, if you see a greyhound walking in a muzzle, please give him space.

Don't get cross if you see a greyhound with a muzzle on, the carers are being responsible and keeping everyone safe and helping to introduce their greyhound to the world in the best way possible. I have known people (myself included) being accused by other dog owners of walking a "dangerous dog". The people that have this attitude are often far more dangerous.

One more thing- if you see a greyhound walking, please do not throw balls for your dog in the direction they are walking, because newly rehomed greyhounds can be surprised very easily and dogs racing towards them chasing balls can cause panic.

It just takes a moment of consideration-they just need a bit of help. Greyhounds are extremely intelligent and very quickly become integrated into their new lives. Other dog owners can either be a huge help or hindrance, and any bad experiences result in increased levels of anxiety for the greyhounds and the people they live with.

If you see a greyhound with a muzzle, please help by allowing them a bit of space. It can make so much difference if you pause for a second or two and allow them to move past before you throw the ball for your dog.

Dopamine drop

Last week I met a friend for a catch up, we were planning to organise some evening activities for the annual summer riding camp. It is fun, and an excuse to have breakfast.
I was looking forward to seeing her as we hadn't met for over 6 months. Over the pandemic months- once we were allowed- we met a few times at a café but before this point our normal place had been Sainsbury's.

We should have stuck with the café because it turned out that Sainsbury's no longer cook anything to order. We were really disappointed as the only available food turned out to be a poor selection that was heated in a microwave. The rolls were delivered, and I was hungry and so busy chatting to her that I didn't really notice what I was eating which was just as well because it tasted of cardboard, even though it was supposed to be egg, spinach and roasted tomatoes.

We planned, took notes, laughed and then parted.
By the time I got home and walked the dogs I was feeling a bit unwell, it was at this point that I realised that the plastic roll was probably responsible for how I felt. This led me to thinking about our dogs. Their mealtimes are often the highlight of their day, just as I had anticipated a lovely breakfast.

How often are dogs given food which may smell appetising to us, but once consumed it does not fulfil all the requirements needed to help them feel satiated. There are many dogs that walk away if their food just doesn't smell or taste good. I have lost count of the times people have complained that their dogs don't eat their food. This may be because our dogs with their heightened sense of

smell are not prepared to eat the equivalent of my breakfast roll. Some foods, especially kibble just do not fulfil the promises on the packet.
It may have the "right" nutrients but lack taste. Eating should be an enjoyable activity.

We might think we *see* behaviour problems, while in the meantime our dogs are feeling queasy and unsatiated. Dogs don't exactly savour their food, and their taste buds don't work quite like ours, but this doesn't prevent us from providing wholesome food that smells good and leaves our dogs licking their bowls out after they have finished. Food affects behaviour and wellbeing, of that there is no doubt. That breakfast roll left me with a headache and feeling slightly nauseous, not to say a little grumpy and disappointed.

Expecting something nice which isn't delivered causes a drop in dopamine. Our brains release dopamine when we anticipate something good but if this is not achieved this results in a dopamine drop, which in turn leads to frustration. This is why food should never be withheld on purpose and why we shouldn't ask our dogs to find food when they are hungry.

Treat searches are a great activity for dogs when they are feeling happy and have had a meal before any nosework activities but they should not replace a meal. Dopamine is an important neurotransmitter which can have profound and far- reaching consequences if a goal is not achieved.

Crossroads

My dogs love a set of crossroads.
There is one particular crossroad they love that is set into a

grassy path which has lots of footfall every day. Every dog that passes by pees, sniffs, inhales and picks up pee mails from other dogs that have previously passed through.

It is a useful area for reactive dogs, including my own lurcher as we have a clear view of who is coming and going and it is a real destination place- from this point the local churchyard can be reached or a short wander leads to some horses and the fields, or the opposite branch leads to the village.

My dogs spend ages there, savouring the smells and messages and they often choose the righthand fork which winds up to the church.

In history crossroads were symbolic for many reasons including mystical ones-and people used to leave warm clothing and useful things for travellers, but they are magical for dogs too!

Grass bathing

It's that time of year, when the grass grows rapidly, and it starts to take on an emerald glow. Before long the mud will disappear and there will be less squelching underneath our feet which will be replaced with areas of lush green and this invites us to pause. This prompts the beginning of a wonderful spring routine, which involves one of my dogs, a chew and some coffee.

We leave the house early in the morning just as the sun starts to become warm and walk to the local churchyard which is a place of serenity. We then find somewhere to sit for 20 minutes, and my greyhound girl chomps on a chew as I sip my coffee. After she has finished, she will seek out an area that has long fronds of grass, lay down, and will select some grass to nibble on as she catches the sun.

I have christened this practice "grass bathing" and from there she watches the squirrels to her hearts content.

What makes this such a special activity is not only because it is so valuable for mental wellbeing but because there is a dog at my side who enjoys it just as much as I do

Fox cub alert!
It is not unusual to see fox cubs around at this time of year, so be especially vigilant when walking in quiet areas like churchyards as you may literally bump into fox cubs playing!
Also don't forget that ***adders*** are likely to be seen as the sun starts to shine.

A Dog For All Seasons

SUMMER

The summer provides us with an opportunity to relax a little. The longer nights and bright mornings give us more time to spend with our dogs and to appreciate their different responses and moods as the sun provides increased warmth. We can plan holidays and extra special walks.

While summer carries a chilled vibe, it can also bring problems including thunder storms and heatwaves, and areas where we have walked our dogs in peace and quiet during colder months can become busy and create problems for anxious or reactive dogs.

However, the positives often outweigh the negatives, and we have freedom to walk well into the evenings and in the early mornings.

"What is this life if, full of care, We have no time to stand and stare. No time to stand beneath the boughs. And stare as long as sheep or cows". Leisure by William Henry Davies

Holidays

When we take our dogs away on holiday, we should always pack and carry a small basic first aid kit. This should include the number of a good local vet nearest to where the holiday is being taken. Please remember that not all vets carry the anti-venom for adder bites, so keep this in mind when choosing areas to walk. The essentials need not be very bulky and are very handy to have around. First and foremost, remember to fill a container of water from home as many dogs dislike the taste of different water, so the water you take with you can help with the transition. Don't forget to include a cool coat because our weather is so unpredictable and they are incredibly useful if the temperatures soar.

Cool coats are also useful if you are camping as it can get chilly art night and they can double up as a extra layer particularly if you have a greyhound as they are prone to get cold at the most inopportune moments.

Greyhounds and many other fine coated dogs including smaller breeds have little body fat and can develop spasms and cramp if they become cold during the night, especially if it has been hot during the day. Camper vans and tents and even holiday cottages can be chilly places!

Suggested basic canine first aid travelling kit

Leucillin/ colloidal silver

Pro-kolin

Tick remover

Tweezers

Vet wrap

Blunt ended scissors

Non adhesive dressing

Small bottle of surgical spirit

Taking a canine first aid course is highly recommended

Safe

I am sure that everyone has different experiences over public holidays. For reactive dogs these holidays can be especially challenging.

The one thing that all reactive dogs need is a *safe space* to stretch their legs and to feel secure. It is really worth looking into areas where you can walk where both you and your dog are able to feel relatively safe from dogs that are running off lead.

Continual exposure to threatening situations does nobody any good, either dogs or their carers. It can take considerable time and energy searching these areas out, and the best way to find suitable areas is to explore on foot *without* your dog. Ideally you need somewhere that you can walk your dog from your house. It really is worth investing time to search these out, because often there are areas right under your nose which people with problem free dogs wouldn't dream of visiting.

The world is still dealing with the situation in Ukraine, so we can all identify with just how important it is to feel safe. A sense of security provides comfort and if a dog has been on high alert, it is vital that balance is established and the body and brain finds a way to recover. Research into the brain shows just how detrimental it is for any of us to be continually on hypervigilant. We lose the capacity to plan and develop strategies and logical thought is impossible.

Flight, fight and freeze reactions are not easy to live with and these reactions can become so normalised for some dogs that there is no way out. Remember that we have little control over these reactions because our autonomic systems are in charge, it may not make sense for a dog to freeze half way across a road but at that point it is unlikely he has a choice over how he is reacting.

This is why developing a degree of confidence is so important, but how can this be achieved when many situations feel so unsafe to many dogs? This leads us back to the search, because if our dogs are always worried and can never really relax, trying to make inroads into reactivity is complex and doomed to failure. It can sometimes seem impossible and improbable that the situation will ever be resolved.

When you search don't dismiss unlikely and unpromising areas including car parks, or tiny grubby areas beside busy roads, or industrial areas. This may not work for dogs that are worried about noise but "ordinary" dog carers are often reluctant to use areas where they can't let their dogs off lead. Leave the more attractive areas for the dogs and owners that are comfortable in any environment- but in actuality many dogs are not as comfortable as their carers believe them to be. These dog owners have fallen into the trap of thinking their dogs should be continually "socialising, and this is one of the reasons why problems with reactivity exist in the first place.

It only takes one negative experience to ruin a dog's life and this can impact so badly that a dog no longer wants to be in close proximity with any other dogs. Continual exposure won't fix anything.

Plan A is to find areas where anxious dogs can explore, and become curious. Curiosity is a huge healer, and signals the return to being able to cope with situations which would otherwise be aversive and destructive. Plan A also involves taking a big step back and beginning with "day zero". Day zero signals a blank canvas and if well planned we can help our dogs to build their confidence from a base level. It consists of asking *nothing* of the dog and this time is used to build trust. Requirements should not be part of the first two weeks of any new regime, and walking outside is not required -even after a specific time if your dog remains unsure consider giving more days off from being in outside areas-apart from your garden- as this can cause more setbacks.

Enrichment and other activities can be put in place instead of walks, and it may even be possible to take a car trip if this is something which is enjoyable to the dog. Without a return to balance within the body we will have to continually and repetitively rely on coping strategies, and while these are essential and provide support we do need a new beginning.

By removing the possibility of continually bumping into other dogs this begins the process of building confidence and is the only way to help a dog to rise above his fears.

Energy. It feels good, doesn't it?

Sometimes in the UK we have heatwaves, and as these high temperatures are not typical many people sleep badly and feel more than a little lacking in energy. Instead of reflecting on this let's take a step back to the nights of more typical temperatures when we wake up and feel joyous. It's pleasant, isn't it? It makes us feel good and we can anticipate a good day. Most of us are lucky because many people have long term illnesses that makes these days particularly special.

What do *we* do with this energy?
We may well do chores, or instead of wasting this precious resource on mundane tasks we might choose to do something which we take pleasure in.

A Dog For All Seasons

This might take the form of a bit of walking, or horse riding, or yoga or we might drive somewhere nice with our dogs. We generally have any number of options open to us on those days, but if we are working, the day is guaranteed to be easy and flies past.

But what if the person you lived with observed your buoyant mood and your open movement and thought that you needed an adrenaline filled half hour that would tire you out? Would this prove to be a positive for you? Weirdly enough this is what many dog carers do when they see that their dogs are full of energy. Many people have a mantra which is a *"tired dog is a good dog,"* or there is an even more worrying sentiment that a tired dog is an obedient dog.

There is so much wrong with this platitude, and one of the labels that I truly detest is "high energy dogs". This phrase often has negative connotations and conversely some people are quite proud of this and point at those of us with slightly more laid- back dogs and tell us how easy our dogs are. The premise is that these high energy dogs need work and lots of exercise which translates that they need to be exercised until they are quiet/ tired/ satiated/ obedient. Pick whatever word you prefer, but whatever word is used means that the ultimate aim is to get rid of the excess energy.

The internet tells me that the opposite of energetic is lethargic. So where does this lead us? It steers us to the point where many people believe that getting rid of excess energy is necessary. It means that dogs have to play or run until they are tired, or until they flop down and sleep.

What happens during fast activities that are ultimately anaerobic in nature is that dogs are unable to sustain this level for long, and because dogs never evolved the ability to sweat this results in physiological challenges for these dogs including the need to stabilise mental and physical balance within the body.

The body has to work hard to lower the heart rate, muscles are likely to ache for a few hours after exercise due to microtrauma in the muscle fibres, and the brain is likely to suffer from free radical and oxidative stress, which quite simply means that anaerobic exercise is damaging and costly to both brain and body, and recovery takes time.

This is very common practice especially for people with puppies and adolescent dogs. This kind of depletion of resources is often seen after prolonged play sessions. Frustration can also result after prolonged exercise.

Energy is different to frustration. If a dog is climbing all over us, or barking at the window, or a puppy is biting it can often signal frustration, but this does not denote that a dog needs more exercise. It might look like the dog is crying out for fast activities but nothing could be further from the truth. It is far more beneficial if we step back and provide more pleasurable and dog centred activities such as allowing them to sniff or to present them with a really nice chew or very radically! actually sit with our dogs and spend some time with them!

Think of the difference between feeling like you could conquer the world and then think of how negative frustration is. There is definitely energy involved in both and we could label it "good" or "bad" energy, but actually let's not. Instead let's begin to understand the difference between a happy and carefree dog that is enjoying his day and one that has multiple frustrations to cope with which **may** look like pent up energy when actually nothing could be further from the truth.

We need to observe our dogs and prevent ourselves from jumping to obvious conclusions which may mean that our dogs suffer from our own misunderstandings and pre- conceptions.

Energy and frustration are different, develop your observational skills and learn to tell one from another.

On Looking

How often do we lose ourselves when we sit and watch something? One of my favourite books is a non- dog one by Alexandra Horowitz called "On Looking".
I often wonder why people don't look up, or even just stand and watch people wandering by. This is something I share with my dogs

They naturally do a lot of sniffing but they also do a lot of watching. One of my greyhounds joins me most mornings at the local churchyard, I take coffee and we just sit and watch things going on around us. She watches the squirrel action and I just take a deep breath and look at the trees and watch the comings and goings of the bees and butterflies and anything else that takes my attention.

If we don't allow our dogs to watch things around them in the environment, we do them a disservice. Dogs need to watch in order to learn about their world, especially when they are young or newly rescued but it is invaluable for all dogs, By observing we can decide whether to move away, engage, or maybe we are just watching to make sense of what is happening ahead, or perhaps we are taking in the view and become lost in what is going on around us.

This may become dated but it is part of the story, last

night I watched the opening ceremony of the Commonwealth games, and as we are all human, we take pleasure in watching specific things, and our dogs are no different, if we don't let our dogs observe the world they are less able to make sense of what is playing out in front of them. If we hurry them along there is a risk that they will begin to react adversely or in fearful ways to everyday things that are of no consequence.

There are exceptions of course, but I often encourage people with anxious or fearful dogs to allow them to watch things, providing they are at an appropriate distance. If they become worried or concerned the carer can quietly move them away but dogs do need to observe their world so they can develop a way of coping and self-regulating their emotions.

If we ask dogs to look at us rather than things that are creating anxiety, we are potentially removing their ability to make sense of what is playing out in front of them and to underline once more, this practice is not always appropriate and judgement is needed but we sometimes need to stand back and watch *them*. Observing and responding to the world around them is crucial in building confidence and helps us to have a better understanding of their communication.

Let your dog have the choice of watching and observing things -from a distance if needs be. Processing and adjusting to what happens around them is better than disturbing a dog if he seems lost in the moment.

Hot, hot, hot

Yes, it can become hot very suddenly, but many people

don't seem to be able to modify their habits when there is a period of hot weather. Rather than adjust to the temperatures they continue to walk their dogs at lunchtime or in the middle of the afternoon. This is ok for most of the year but a change in behaviour is *essential* when the weather is hot.

This is especially important for the short- nosed breeds or dogs that have little or no insulation including sighthounds but any dog can die *quickly* in excessive heat. Dogs have little ability to regulate their own temperatures when weather becomes hot, they can sweat through their pads and lose heat through panting but that is about it.

How would it feel on a hot day if we were unable to sweat and stuck with two layers which couldn't be removed? Especially if forced to exercise at the hottest point of the day. Add to this the effect of the sympathetic system which will switched to high as temperatures climb all combine to create a perfect storm for our dogs. The ANS (Autonomic nervous system) does this to enable us to cope with extreme heat, but this can add to the burden and make both us and our dogs a bit short tempered.

Dogs are far more likely to react badly by biting, growling or biting in conditions when they are trying to keep themselves cool so leave them be!
With this in mind how can we help them?

- Keep walks to the coolest part of the day
- Make sure dogs have access to lots of cool water
- Use a cool coat which must be kept wet at all times when used. Never allow a cool coat to dry out if a dog is wearing one.
- Ice cubes can be dropped into water bowls to melt

- Ground is rock hard too, so stick to slow activities. Legs and feet quickly become sore and heat stroke *will* kill.

If you suspect heat stroke

Be vigilant - heat stroke is deadly and will kill in an incredibly short time, if you observe any of the symptoms listed please get your dog to the vet immediately

Temperature of 39.4C or above, rapid breathing, heavy panting, and dramatically raised heart rate, excessive drooling, bright red gums and tongue, drooling, skin which is hot to the touch or having difficulty standing.

If the above are accompanied by a seizure it will be almost impossible to save your dog's life, please do not take risks during days of excessive heat.

Sea water poisoning

Dogs have also been known to die as a result of ingesting salt water. While a small amount is unlikely to cause a problem, the symptoms can look almost identical to heat stroke but are as life threatening so do make sure you keep a careful eye on your dog if you visit the beach even on a cool day.

Heat hangover

Has the weather been significantly warmer than normal? If so, how did you sleep? Did you have a restless night? The optimum temperature for humans to get good sleep is apparently 18 degrees C but that possibly varies a little for most of us.

It is difficult for most of us to sleep in unusual heat, at

least until we are acclimatised to it, and because temperatures fluctuate so much in the UK it is hard to adjust to. This results in disturbed sleep patterns and prevents us getting the "right" kind of sleep and leaves us feeling gritty eyed and less rational. This is exactly the same for our dogs, and just like us, dogs can suffer from sleep deprivation with all the negatives that brings, and they can be particularly affected by the heat.

Last night I came in from the garden once it was dark after enjoying the cool of the evening to find that I seemed to be missing a dog. This made me sigh as the only place she could possibly be would be on the bed. I usually love my greyhound sleeping on the bed but I can almost guarantee she will choose to sleep upstairs on the hottest nights of the year. She of course always gets a bit terse with me which results in us both sleeping badly.

I have yet to understand why she would rather sleep upstairs in the sauna rather than remain downstairs in the cool, but nevertheless for some reason it has become a habit for her.

Always make allowances for dogs if the temperatures have been high as they are likely to feel groggy and out of sorts, just as we are. Short tempers are not the only result of the heat-it is common for dogs to refuse food until temperatures are lower. Prepare to be flexible during and after any heat waves

An evening saunter

In mid winter I look back to the summer with a longing. As I walk my dogs I try to find bonuses and positives about being out on freezing cold mornings or during dark soggy evenings. I would always prefer to be outside than inside but I loathe the winter with a passion. I hate the sharp winds that feel like they are going to freeze my eyelashes to my face, and I resent the many layers of clothing that I need when the temperature drops, and as the dogs pause to sniff and take in the scents, I stamp my feet and dream of warmer days.

These are the days. I know many people don't like the summer but I adore it. I especially love spending the evenings sauntering along as the dogs pause to pick up a scent, I love watching their bodies move without the layers they need during the winter that inevitably restrict their movement

The evenings and mornings bring different scents and it seems as if the world just pauses to take a breath too. When we think of the seasons with regard to our dogs it must seem to them that the summers are long and are here just for them. I often spend more time with my dogs in the garden, although it is tiny and while they are all rarely outside together, if I sit and write in the cool of the evening, there is always one dog outside listening to the sounds and sharing the warm air with me.

The year must seem odd to our dogs and it must speed up during the hectic bits and slow down rapidly at other points. Christmas and New Year must be intolerable to them as we dash around preparing for whatever festivities we get involved in. The speeding up and slowing down must seem incomprehensible. But we can breathe a sigh of relief that we have room before the mornings start to become darker and we lose the evening saunter times.

Its lovely to spend extra time just watching and moving slowly and remain present as the dogs explore the varying smells as the summer progresses. The scent of May must be so different to the scents that occur after the fields have been harvested- we know that our dogs have an amazing sense of smell and it is possible to ponder on just how amazing that sense is. Do they- for example- have the ability to pick up distant scents from the countryside if they live in the city or vice versa? We as humans have little knowledge or understanding of the kind of detail and depth that their sense of smell might convey to them so maybe they are able to pick up novel scents from many miles away in specific conditions

Saunter and savour the summer evenings. Pick blackberries and forage and help your dogs to participate because these are the true dog days of summer

Holiday cover

How do our dogs cope when we are away?
This thought crept into my mind after I had been away for a few days because I was a little bothered about how my dogs responded when I got home. My brother had very kindly agreed to look after them while I was away, but he is not a dog person, the arrangement was not ideal but it was the best solution at that point in time.

When I arrived home, they were all very calm, I pottered about unpacking and they mostly draped themselves over the sofas while I considered the effect of having a stranger in the house. How were they really feeling? Calm, tired or something else? Because there seemed to be another emotion present. They were not quite themselves.

The morning after bought some thoughts on this. They had only met my brother a few times so my reflections revolved around that fact. If a relative stranger came to your house without a previous explanation, and started doing random things like making tea, sleeping upstairs and doing what humans do there is no doubt it would be quite creepy.

This would undoubtedly explain my dogs' response of looking a little tired and deflated when I returned home. Having a relatively unknown person in the house must have been very weird and their world must of felt out of their control. We are the advocates for our dogs, and I know many people would dismiss this as being bonkers but my dogs are my best friends, so it is up to me to do better the next time I need to leave them.

Were they ok? Yes. Did they get food? Yes. But their state of mind was slightly disturbed, they must have been relieved when they saw me walk through the door. I think this is something we all have to think about if we take time away from our dogs, no matter how qualified or dog savvy the people you choose to look after your dogs' may be.

Foraging?

There are many people that live with dogs that don't understand why foraging would be so enjoyable for them. I often watch people marching their dogs along and refusing to allow them to sniff, so foraging would most definitely be out of the question. Yet it is such a lovely pastime.

I am not saying that dogs should be encouraged to eat old chicken bones or rubbish thrown out of their car windows, but I would like to highlight how pleasurable it is for dogs to be given the chance to forage for nice things.

I know how much I enjoy this time of year. Foraging for blackberries, is especially enjoyable because it is a special activity including picking the ones that are just out of reach, studying the hedgerows and then learning which berries are ripe and how they taste. Even the ones that look just perfect can be sour, it always reminds me of the Harry Potter books, as it can be a bit like choosing a "Bertie botts every flavour bean" because you never quite know what a berry is going to taste like. Most of all it is a wonderful way of sending an hour with your dog.

Enrichment activities are essential for dogs. Foraging is particularly enjoyable and is a simple thing to share, dogs often approach it with interest and curiosity and we should encourage them to experiment and investigate too. Dogs love choice but don't always need us to put a selection of items out for them when there are things that are available in the environment and opportunities already exist where they can search for their own treasure.

If we set up things that look correct and pleasing to ourselves this is not always as enjoyable for our dogs because they can be unnatural and less inviting for their canine senses. Dogs love to experiment and leave things and then perhaps return to what was initially dismissed, this might be because maybe it was a little difficult to reach or perhaps less tasty or perhaps the dog decided that the scent needed to be investigated at leisure later on.

Foraging activities are not tasks they should be pleasures which are on offer every day

After the rain

Petrichor is a lovely word for the smell that is left after it rains. The term was coined by Australian scientists in 1964 to describe the unique, *earthy smell associated with rain*. It is caused by the water from the rain, along with certain compounds like ozone, geosmin, and plant oils in the soil.

Our dogs are of course ahead of us as far as any changes in scents and smells are concerned and will stick their heads down or into the wind to make the most of any scents. Dogs often delight in in a bit of puddle paddling and jumping too, the fresh water can be really inviting and refreshing but do be aware that puddles can contain toxins and bacteria

The rain can often signal positive changes in the behaviour of most dogs. They may seem more energised, more interested and despite these changes this can result in increased relaxation if we make sure that we don't assume that just because the temperature drops that it is time to step up the exercise.

Enjoy the cool and let your dog take the lead.

Snakes and ladders

I don't know how many people know about this board game, but it was pretty popular when I was a kid which was a very long time ago! As I walk with my lurcher and negotiate the paths and areas I often have to backtrack and scramble over places I would rather not be as he spies yet another dog. I call it his "spidey sense" as he often knows dogs are around long before I do.

He is anxious about meeting other dogs and really dislikes being close to unfamiliar dogs. I have realised in my quest to provide good walks for him that he is fine with other "pointy noses" and this is why his anxiety was never picked up on when he was in rescue, as it specialises in lurchers and greyhounds. Sometimes it takes a while to understand why a specific rescue or shelter organization may be unable to provide input on specific areas of behaviour.

Returning to our walks, they are varied. There are the good walks, the ones where we don't have to backtrack and cross fields and hide behind hedges and there are the bad ones where people just don't get it even though, apparently, they are themselves truly gifted with knowledge of all dogs and what they need.

One woman offered advice one day to a client of mine and told her that someone had solved his dog's reactivity by getting him to hold a ball in his mouth while walking. Apart from the problems which may result from over shadowing this is no way of solving the problems that a fearful dog may have.

The snakes and ladders game helps us to evaluate the distance we need between us and other dogs when walking. It gives the sensible dog walkers that don't have dogs with problems themselves information on how to handle a situation that is in front of them, and with luck they will clip their own dogs on lead and are cautions about how near they are.

Fear is rubbish. Only the other day I had the most detailed nightmare, I couldn't get it off my mind, and during that week I found myself inventing scenarios that could lead into the situation I saw in my dream. It wasn't a nice thing to have following me around and it is likely that my brain was changing and the fear area (the amygdala) was expanding to accommodate my fears.

Fear is held in the brain and the body. To those fearful dogs that can't bear to be near dogs, people, or even cars it is a living nightmare.

Snakes and ladders are necessary. One step forward, one step back, some positive and some negative, but we need to be prepared to step in if our dogs need help.

Proprioception

Proprioception is defined as "the perception or awareness of the position and movement of the body".
It is important that we understand what it is and how it can be integrated into walks. Proprioception is one of the senses that we all possess and is as important to wellbeing as sight, smell and hearing. Being able to balance and move with ease is integral to health

As far as our dogs are concerned doing exercises that aim to help them with their balance and proprioception, will only be of benefit if we understand and facilitate the following points

- Dogs should choose and consciously decide where to place their feet and bodies and have the choice to avoid doing what is uncomfortable
- Luring a dog into position is not a benefit. Food is a big motivator for dogs and it is possible that they may be so focused on food that they are not consciously thinking about what they are doing.
- If asked to perform a particular task such as climbing onto or over an obstacle it involves the brain and in particular the cerebellum. This is an important area of the brain, it has complex functions but a google search will tell you that it is involved with movement

If we think about the placement of our own feet as we are walking and concentrate on what is happening as we step onto grass or from grass to tarmac or from short grass to long grass it is incredibly beneficial.

Different textures that are underneath our feet combine to give our bodies and brains a lot of information.

It can also *feel* good, especially moving from a hard surface onto a soft surface. Our brains are activated as we walk and are busy regulating our balance. Children often delight in climbing onto walls and walking along them as do many dogs, this is all about choice and pleasure.

   This is what proprioception is about. What it is **not** about is luring dogs into position onto areas and then giving a command to stay put for a prescribed time. There does not have the huge benefits for the brain and body that free choice brings. Proprioception is about co-ordinating the vestibular, tactile and visual senses which leads to integration of the senses and helps with processing sensory information.

The right kind of activity should not be too difficult for a dog to do. If there is a small problem to solve while walking it will combine with the other senses and come up with a solution and help our dogs to live longer and happier lives

Morning muse.

I have been writing an article for a dog magazine over the last week or so, sometimes they take me ages and I have to scrap most of it and sometimes they are really easy to write and words just come together in a very satisfying way. This month has been a difficult one for many reasons, but my dogs are always here, they are always present and I am lucky to have them.

A Dog For All Seasons

If I have no energy or enthusiasm for anything much, they are happy to provide amazing companionship and I have to thank my lovely older greyhound for being my muse as we wander in the mornings. The early sunny mornings are the best, we can stretch out in the sun settle, and appreciate sitting in the lovely churchyard. I often wonder how different the times we share are in comparison to other people who have dogs.

I know from looking at social media that humans are impatient, and want the "perfect dog". In my experience we are far from perfect so how we can expect dogs to be "perfect" is beyond me, especially as they are a different species too us and have a different ethogram.

What do these people expect when they use punitive methods to address what they see as "problem behaviours"?

What part of a healthy puppy that bounds around the house picking things up with joyous abandon is wrong especially if he has been isolated at night in a crate? Why are we humans so critical?

Too many people resort to harsh methods to "correct" what is seen as bad behaviour when it is in fact part of the ethogram of the species that we ***choose*** to live with.
A grasp of what is natural and normal for dogs really needs to be highlighted before people buy a puppy. If they were aware of what is natural for a dog, perhaps they wouldn't decide to bring a dog into their lives. Canine wellbeing and the basic needs of dogs need to be understood rather than criticised and punished. Dogs are dogs, we can't and shouldn't try to change them into Disney characters. Only a few days ago I read a comment, I have no idea where but it went something like this

A Dog For All Seasons

"Dogs weren't domesticated by humans, they domesticated us"
Water

Water should always be available to your dog, especially when it is hot but is it important that it is fresh water? The reason for the question is that it takes hours before the chemicals that are in our water get to a point where they are less potent, so it may be that water needs to stand for a while before it is tolerable to our dogs. I have known this information for ages, so I let my dogs to make the decision as to which they prefer by leaving two bowls for them. One bowl is "older" water that has been standing longer and the other contains fresh water. From my observations I have to say that my dogs often choose the fresher water.

I assume they are so used to the chemical smell that they would rather have it straight from the tap but the choice is always available. Always keep an eye on dehydration, it is one of the things that can lead to a huge deterioration in health.
This can be checked by picking up a tiny bit of your dog's skin on his neck and then letting go. It should spring back immediately. If it doesn't and stays as a little raised tent for more than a second or two your dog is dehydrated.

There are dogs that drink very little but manage to stay hydrated and dogs that drink immense amounts, it just depends on the individual. Unless a huge change is seen in the amounts that your dog drinks from day to day-unless it is hot -there should be no cause for concern.
Another thing to ponder on is what your dogs' bowls are made from. It is now widely understood that cheap plastic bowls should be avoided particularly if they are being used

for water, as they have been shown to leach *BPA's (Bisphenol-A.)* There are also possible links to this chemical being able to mimic the effect of oestrogen in the body leading to weight gain and hormone imbalance.

Neither should A*luminium* bowls be used for water or feeding bowls as there are possible links to kidney and brain diseases. It is far safer to use china or stainless steel as bowls for dogs.

There is also the potential for your dog to pick up small electric shocks when thunder is around from metal objects such as bowls so choose with care.

Outside is best!

Over the last few years a few things have become apparent to me. One of the most important is that dogs and puppies learn so much better when they are outside.

I don't really know where the preoccupation started with teaching puppies in halls. Halls have slippery floors, sounds echo and voices ricochet around the area. Then there are often constant interruptions before the class begins as doors are opened and puppies arrive, people talking and chairs scraping on the floors.

When I was at school many years ago, I remember the odd lesson which was given outside. It was a real treat to feel the sun on my back, and have the sounds and scents of nature around. I still look back on these lessons with fondness even though they probably didn't happen more than half a dozen times.

This leads to the question as to why we teach the most important things to our dogs inside halls? They often contain unnatural scents including the chemicals which are used for cleaning. How much of the dog's senses are taken up with these impressions which compete against the process of learning?

I have run indoor classes. I never enjoyed them. I used to worry that there was always one puppy that would feel uncomfortable and hide behind the chair that the carer was sat in. People are not comfortable in static positions either, and some people have not been in a classroom setting since they left school, and become frustrated if the puppies are unable to settle. Even if class members remembered to bring beds for their puppy, they were rarely comfortable enough to settle in an alien environment.

Life skills are so much easier to teach outside, plus people need to understand how to teach their puppy in natural environments. For instance, I used to have many conversations with people about how difficult it was to recall their puppies outside even when the recalls they did in class were perfect.

Then there is the thorny issue of dog communication and how to tell which dogs are friendly and safe to introduce a puppy to and which ones should be avoided. When we are outside, it is easy to point out dog communication and advise on body postures that other dogs exhibit as we are moving around during class. This empowers the dog carers and helps them steer clear of bad interactions and they are in a better place to advocate for their dogs.

Recall might be harder to teach outdoors but if help is available, it highlights the skills that are needed. People often ask their puppies to recall over distances that are too long, or they call repeatedly when the puppy is having a quiet sniff, or they make bad decisions about where and when to let puppies off lead. This can all be addressed during outside classes.

Outside is natural, it has huge advantages for dogs and their guardians and we all need to experience the different conditions and situations that may occur when we are out with our dogs

This applies equally to older dogs too, if we need to teach essentials like walking on a loose lead and the basics of recall then these skills can be more successfully tutored in carefully selected and quiet outside areas.

Dog farts

No apologies are offered for including this section! I think we are all acquainted with that moment where you want to grab a cushion and smother your face as a blast of noxious gas reaches your nostrils and your dog looks at you in puzzlement.

There is no doubt flatulence can be a source of amusement and I have heard every quip from various dog carers as to why this situation occurs. Often people put it down to very rich food, but I have my reservations as to whether this is true. Certainly, it might excuse the odd human trump but we all know which foods are likely to cause us problems and with this knowledge we might decide to avoid a particular food, but why people are so blasé about their dog's internal workings has always puzzled me. These are not my words but from something I found on the internet:

"The most common cause of flatulence is a change in diet or from the dog eating something spoiled (dietary indiscretion)".

Most cases of chronic flatulence are caused by a diet that is poorly digested by the dog. These poorly digestible diets cause excessive fermentation in the colon and subsequent gas formation.

If this is so, why do people carry on feeding their dogs a diet that they know their dogs find difficult to digest? Sometimes people seem quite proud of having shopped around and found a food that is reputed to be "very high quality" and then proceed to feed it to their dog but are oblivious to the effects it has on them.

Farting can often accompany sounds from our dog's stomachs which have the glorious name of *borborygmus*. But these sounds are not normal, and we should understand that farting accompanied with a rumbling gurgling stomach is not funny for a dog. These are often the consequence of our dogs sharing our takeaway food such as curries, It's not that dogs should never share our food, but it is not fair to feed foods that create stomach distension and pain within the dogs GI tract.

If farting is a common occurrence rather than a rarity, it needs to be investigated. Obviously, dogs will often eat what is offered to them and they are certainly opportunistic about scavenging because this is the nature of a dog, but it is worth understanding that GI problems are not necessarily caused by feeding grains, however many people think they are the culprit. Whatever the cause we cannot expect dogs to thrive on diets which are indigestible.

It may not be that your dog is actually allergic to an ingredient in a food, but more likely it will be due to quality. Intolerance of an ingredient is often far more common than an actual allergy so there is a distinction between the two.

If your dog is an inveterate farter a bit of investigation is needed to put things right

Dogs in transit

During the summer most of us will want or need to take our dogs somewhere in a car. This is not a problem for the majority of dogs but there are some considerations we might need to think about before we take our dogs anywhere.

The most important concern is safety. Most people have well designed and safe ways in which to transport their dogs but not everyone. While it can be quite amusing to see a dog with his head hanging out of a car window when it is moving, it most certainly is not safe. The dog may enjoy it but there are way too many risks involved and we should prevent our dogs from being able to do this at all costs.

This probably comes down to educating owners into making good decisions for their dogs, but sometimes the transport the dogs are in is just not suitable. This does not mean you have to spend way over your budget to get a car to suit your dog, as most cars can be made dog friendly and safe with a bit of time and knowledge.

There are many dogs that are nervous about travelling in cars. They may have had a bad experience, or not travelled in a car before being bought home. This is obviously the case with puppies and many do get travel sick for the first month or so when they initially go home. The standard advice in regard to puppies is to have two people present when making the first journey. One person should drive, and the other should sit in the back with the puppy safely beside them. This provides comfort and can help with any distress a puppy might experience.

As with any new experiences a puppy can become

worried or frightened and it can take many months before any negative associations are resolved. First experiences are important and need to be pleasant. The first car journey is a big event as it is also combined with being the first ever time a puppy has left his siblings and his mother, so he will be confused, worried and the whole experience must be terrifying, so careful planning is needed in order to provide a puppy with a positive experience

Make sure you have some water from your puppy's previous home to offer him if you stop along the way. Odd smelling water can prevent a puppy drinking and cause dehydration. Apart from the upset of leaving his family, puppies are more likely to suffer from car sickness because the areas of the inner ear which are involved in balance are not fully developed. This normally resolves itself around a year of age.

Older dogs can find car journeys distressing too. Not many people suffer from travel sickness, but if they do they have a preference as to where they sit in a car. Obviously, this is not an option for a travel- sick dog that needs to be in the back of a car for safety reasons. However, cars can be noisy smelly places especially the back of the car. Besides this there is a lot of sensory input when travelling.

The sensation of speed, for instance, compounds feelings of confinement from which there is no escape, and one of my own dogs becomes very agitated when cars come towards us. He feels more comfortable on motorways when the traffic is all moving in the same direction, but if we are travelling on normal roads I have to drive quite slowly as this seems to disturb him less. Even sun shades on the back windows don't really block out his discomfort, although these can be a really good precaution and help reduce direct sunlight and minimise heat in a car during summer months.

Some dogs refuse to sit or lay down. Standing up in a car can cause problems from constantly becoming unbalanced and create muscle imbalances which then lead to atrophy and stiffness. It is worth starting from scratch in this scenario and trying to find out how you can put your dog more at ease. Sometimes a smaller area helps to settle these dogs, and sometimes they need a larger area.

Make sure your dog does not feel either too hot or too cold when travelling as this can certainly have an impact. If you consider how your dog feels as he travels you can then minimise bad experiences and avoid heightened stress levels.

If problems are directly related to travel sickness there are a few remedies worth trying. Be aware that if you are thinking about using essential oils, or any kind of calming wipes, it is important to check with your dog first before you place them in your car.

Don't flood a dog with a specific scent just on the premise that it has been recommended to you. Not all dogs are able to tolerate specific essential oils, even if they help *us* to feel calmer. There are certain smells that we can't tolerate, but we should all be aware that a dogs' sense of smell is much more heightened than a humans, especially if it is to be used in the confined area of a car.

To check if the scent is going to be of use hold the bottle of the oil/ wipe/ smell you are considering using towards your dogs' nose, if he dislikes it, he will turn his head away and refuse to inhale and this will inform you that this should not be used. Having pointed this out, there may well be oils which will be beneficial, so do consult a zoopharmacognosy therapist to make sure you are supporting your dog in the right way.

As we are discussing smells within a car, please do avoid using synthetic car fragrances. If you are currently using one, please put it in the bin, this can in itself create a reluctance to get into the car.

If your dog is persistently car sick make an appointment with your vet and find out if there are any medications which might relieve motion sickness, and while there, ask the vet to check for any inner ear or vestibular problems which might be causing discomfort.

Other options that are worth looking into are homeopathy or herbs but as previously discussed the first step is to ask a vet to check for any physical problems and then approach people with a professional knowledge of herbs and homeopathy.

Quiet training can be started after ruling out pain and discomfort but will need to be broken down into easy steps to take the fear and worry out of car travel.
There are other things which people have used with success before a car journey, like specific foods which help with digestion, but do leave at least an hour between feeding your dog and travelling.

As our dogs age, we may need to consider how they get in and out of a car. Ramps can be a very good solution but they do need to be sturdy and wide enough so they don't bend underneath the weight of the dog. But, before this point is reached. please do pay attention to how your dog gets in and out of a car. It is recommended that cars are parked next to a curb or step so dogs don't need to stretch or over reach especially when the weather is cold. Similarly getting *out* of a car can damage front legs, necks and backs if a drop is too steep. Parking next to a soft area of grass can help or carry something in your car like a yoga mat for your dog to jump down onto as this will help lessen concussion and cushion the landing and help prevent damage to joints, shoulders and back muscles.

There are indeed lots of considerations when travelling even short distances and safety is of prime importance. Monitor your dog carefully to ensure he is comfortable because bad associations when travelling can stop dogs enjoying trips which should otherwise be full of joy and pleasure.

Extinct!

This popped into my mind a few days ago as I was wandering one morning with my greyhound on our morning muse. I think dogs are resourceful, capable and have evolved to be specialised at scavenging and foraging and these natural behaviours ensure they could live without us.

Dogs have special survival skills and are naturally social, there would be breeds that would find it difficult but these are the ones that have been bred to look a particular way. The breeds with shortened faces have a price to pay as this creates change to the pelvic area which results in restriction of their movement and inability to give birth naturally. But this is the result of human greed and idiocy and has nothing to do with natural selection. Arguably most dogs would cope really well.

They have evolved to scavenge, are very sociable and the current reactive dogs would do their thing and pair up with other dogs they felt safe with, and they would sleep on the outskirts of any group so that could move away if the need occured. They would regain proper sleep without our interference and puppies could stay longer with their mothers and form good solid social connections and remain with their siblings if they chose to.

Breeds as we know them would gradually disappear and adapt to the terrain within the areas they lived in and according to available food.

There would be natural stressors but dogs are well set up to cope with those, play would be spontaneous and natural and not assisted with balls or other human inventions. Exercise would look very different and serve a useful purpose in hunting and forming social affiliations, and it is unlikely that they would be moving at great speed for very long.

This can be speculated on as we know about the canine ethogram, and the point is that dogs are admirably equipped to live in the world, it is humans that complicate their lives.

Do our dogs need us? Only if they live in our world.

Dogs and horses

You are far more likely to come across horses at this time of year because riders take advantage of the long evenings and light mornings just as dog walkers do. Horses can be ridden in hot weather because they are able to regulate their temperature through sweating, but many riders prefer to ride in the cool as it is far more enjoyable and they often ride before or after work as the light is so good.

Be vigilant if horses are likely to be in the areas that you use for walks. There are areas where riders have little

choice of where to ride and one of the pleasures of owning a horse is hacking. This can bring dog walkers and horse riders into conflict. Never forget that horses are prey animals and are likely to bolt when they are scared.
Not only can they bolt *away* from dogs but also *towards* them so be aware that they are easily startled and can become frightened far faster than you may comprehend

Dogs can be particularly worrying for horses as their eyes are at the front of their faces and this signals a potential predator, and dogs are more likely to be identified as carnivores as they smell of meat. Dogs are not the only animals with a hugely enhanced senses and horses can be on instant alert if dogs are moving fast in the near distance. If your dog sees a horse do not expect him to be calm if he has no experience of them.

If you know you are walking in an area where horses are frequently seen, keep your dog on a long line unless you your dogs recall is 100% or unless your dog is very well acquainted with horses. Many horse owners have dogs so they are very comfortable around them- in the case of my own greyhounds they came from a rescue where they walk in fields full of horses everyday-which is really helpful as they pay little attention to horses- but this is not the case for most dogs.

If you spot horses when you are out, please don't climb into trees or bushes in order to help because this can be frightening and spook a horse. Instead put your dog on a lead and stand quietly or walk in the opposite direction. This teaches dogs to be calm around horses and it helps the riders who are always truly appreciative of any help. Young horses in particular are curious but are also lacking in wordly experience, although you are unlikely to be able to tell a young horse from an older one if you are not familiar with them, please do give all horses space.

Never forget horses *will* kick first and think later. Please don't risk yourself, your dog or put a horse or rider in danger by allowing your dog to run around a horse whether he is being ridden or at leisure in a field

A picnic with your dog.

Summer is a great time to plan an adventure with your dog and if you include a picnic, it is even better. A picnic can be combined with a road trip or alternatively just pack a few things into a bag for your dog and yourself and walk somewhere local.

The best areas combine sun and shade, perhaps a stream or a place where the terrain has logs and different surfaces and places which are infused with scents and natural sounds where you can wander, and let your dog sniff and take in the sights and sounds of the area.

As far as a dog picnic is concerned think about what your dog really enjoys eating.

You could do a consumer test a few days before you plan the trip. The way you might do this is as follows- Start with 3 or 4 different foods. The list might include

1) Cheese
2) Liver
3) Chicken
4) Sausages
5) Vegetables, yes, some dogs do love carrots for example.

To do the test, have a pencil and paper on hand to list the

order of selection

Pick two of the foods you have assembled, but be careful not to handle both foods in both hands. Put a little of each food in each hand, and close your fist, this is just to make clear to your dog that he has to choose which he would like to eat first, and hold both your hands out towards your dog.

Let him sniff and choose, it will be obvious which one your dog wants to sample as he will nuzzle that hand with his nose or use a paw.

Whichever is selected first becomes number 1)

Pick another 2 different treats after you have thoroughly washed your hands – this takes the smell away of the foods you previously had in your hands. (If your hands still smell of the original food you may not end up with the most favourite foods).

Continue to work your way through the selection until you have the ones your dog picked first from each taste test. Finally hold the favourites out in the same way to get the very "favourite of favourites"!

Having outlined the principals of a taste test, you could bake a few treats for your dog, they usually love sardines so below is a simple sardine cake recipe that actually tastes pretty good for people too, especially if you add a bit of butter or a spread of your choice.

A recipe for sardine cake

1 cup of plain flour
1 tablespoon baking powder
2 large eggs

1 425g tin of sardines

Mix flour, baking powder and eggs and the fish together, put into a tin or muffin cases put in the oven at 180 degrees and cook for about 25 minutes.
I can guarantee your dogs will love it!

Blueberry treats
Ingredients
1 cup of Blueberries
1 cup of oats
1 cup of whole wheat flour
2 eggs
1 cup of Peanut butter -*but make sure it is xylitol free* (More expensive brands are best as they only contain peanuts).
½ cup warm water

Pre heat oven to 180 degrees
Put blueberries in a mixing bowl and smash them up a little, or you can cut them up if they are fresh.
Add the oats and mix them up with the blueberries.
Add the flour, peanut butter a tiny bit of salt.
Mix together and then add 1/2 cup of warm water, so it sticks together in a doughy ball. (You won't need to use as much water if you are using frozen blueberries)
Roll out the dough to about ½ inch thick, then cut out the treats with a cookie cutter or any shape you fancy, put them on a non- stick baking tray, and bake for 40 minutes.

Both these recipes are great for dogs or us!

Relax with your dog
Devote some time over the long days to relax with your dog – perhaps take a trip where you can share fish and chips, which is a lovely way of spending a sunny summers evening enjoying a bit of quality time with your dog.

A Dog For All Seasons

AUTUMN

Autumn is a time of glorious golden, warm colours which are embraced by many, but it can be one of the most difficult times of the year for dogs.
Halloween and the firework season can bring many aspects that dogs find hard to cope with.

There is a special section at the end of this chapter to help you manage how you in turn can help your dog if he sufferers from firework effects, like many thousands of other dogs.

"Curiosity conquers fear"

Have you ever thought about how Autumn affects your dog?

The seasons are changing, and darkness is encroaching. Once upon a time I had a lurcher that suffered from SAD (Seasonal Affective Disorder). His mood would drop every autumn as the darkness increased and the days grew colder. Part of the solution was to give him rescue remedy and take him out to places that he enjoyed at every opportunity to help lift his mood.

There are many different Bach flower remedies but in his case rescue remedy worked well so this is often my "go to" when my dogs are upset. I've not had a dog since that seemed to suffer quite as badly, but the transition was so clear. Once Spring rolled around again, he became a much happier dog.

At this point in the year the days get shorter but human social activities seem to increase with the approach of

Halloween and Christmas. These can impact negatively on our dogs, so we need to be aware of how we can help minimise the disruption to their lives. There may be rapidly escalating excitement levels if children are in the house, especially if they like to dress up in costumes. Please do consider your dog if there are any celebrations in and around your house or in the local area.

Rapidly on the tail of Halloween is "Firework season" and many dogs become very anxious and worried. Some supermarkets are refusing to sell fireworks, but despite this there's no doubt that it is hard to escape them.

Have you noticed your dog's stress levels shooting up rapidly at this time of year? Try to pick up on any changes in your dog's behaviour. Think carefully if your dog begins to mark in the house, or is reluctant to leave the safety of home and make sure you are kind to your dog, even if behaviour is bizarre and you don't understand the changes. These could include actively avoiding being touched or becoming very picky with food.

It is our job as dog carers to notice and pick up on these changes and to support our dogs. Among the assistance we can provide is to increase the amount of time we spend with them, and it is a really great time to take a holiday with your dog. Many locations offer special rates during Autumn so it's a great treat to get away as the weather changes.

Human posture and dogs

Can human posture impact on dogs?

What might dogs feel if they are in close proximately with someone who has a stooped posture or a person that is unsteady on their feet, and in particular what effect might this have on a dog that has just moved into a new home?

There has to be a question as to whether a dog is able to feel relaxed if someone in the house is compromised in some way. If I were lower to the floor, and was unable to move, it would make me nervous if someone near me appeared to be unsteady and unpredictable as they moved around. This is likely to be uncomfortable for most dogs, but particularly if the dog has recently been rehomed or is compromised himself in some way.

A dog that has just moved into a new home will have a different reaction to this kind of situation to that of a dog that already lives with people whose health is gradually declining but he is already familiar and feel safe with. A newly rehomed dog is likely to feel uncomfortable interacting with anyone he perceives as unpredictable. Rescue dogs often suffer from anxiety and it can be difficult to pinpoint exactly what is causing a dog to feel vulnerable or unsure, but it is worth considering people within a new home.

Dogs can sometimes react to people in hats or dark clothing, but it is worth reflecting on whether they may also be responding to the posture and body language of unfamiliar people. It's also important to remember that scent can have negative as well as positive associations for our dogs.

Dogs have an amazing sense of smell and are able to detect illnesses like cancer, as well as alerting the people they live with to an oncoming epileptic fit for example.

Dogs can also respond negatively to children if they are excited, so there is a similar chance that they are likely to have a reaction to unpredictable movement in adults which may produce cascades of emotion in a dog.

If a dog does react with uncertainty to someone, it's important to respect the dog's reluctance to engage. This is the time of year that humans begin to wear extra layers of clothes. Restrictive clothing changes how people move, and can smell of being stored away from fresh air for many months, which can result in sensory overload. These visual and olfactory elements in the environment can be of concern to many dogs.

It's important to allow your dog to move away if he is visibly unnerved around you or anyone you meet, however well you may know the dog yourself.

Scars

Many of our dogs have scars due to injury or surgery, but some rescue dogs have far deeper scars from incidents which occurred in their previous lives. This is easily overlooked, and even if pinpointed, it's unlikely that we know how they were sustained. It has to be accepted that at least some scars are the result of abuse, or trauma.

Scars can create misery. Many of us have scars, as an example, I have one on my knee, which is the result of a break. I had surgery and plates and pins inserted into it directly after the accident which were removed at a later date, but a scar still remains. One side is still numb even after many years, but it doesn't affect me, or cause any problems. This may not be so with dogs. Even tiny scars can be reminders of a traumatic past event.

Scars may look tiny on the outside, but may go deep into the surrounding tissue and create a corkscrew of fibrous tissue and fascia. Scar tissue is unlike normal tissue and forms adhesions to deep structures around it, which are unable to be seen on the surface. With regard to our dogs, we need to consider that these areas may cause restriction or feel uncomfortable.

An example of this is a client's greyhound, he has a huge scar on his shoulder which was sustained through a bad injury when he was younger. The scars aren't particularly visible, but the adhesions underneath can be clearly felt. Without doubt these have a direct effect on his movement and comfort, combining to make him very guarded, which in turn clearly dent his confidence.

Many people are emotional about their scars and some may feel nauseous if the scar is touched. Not only can scars create physical restrictions but they can also prompt a myriad of emotions if touched. Keep this in mind if you have a dog with scars, however small. If you have a dog that dislikes being touched it may be because there are scars yet to be discovered. So, if your dog is defensive about a specific area of his body take a careful look, but be cautious as you check.

There is such a thing as "scar work" and body work therapists are often able to help with this. It's possible to learn basic scar work which can help alleviate some of the physical and emotional discomfort. It is gentle, non - manipulative and may prove beneficial to many dogs that suffer from adhesions.

"Busy, busy"

Have you ever thought about the fact that dogs are the only animals that have to tell us when they need to toilet?

A Dog For All Seasons

This is especially of concern when supporting puppies. Many people are obsessed about house training their puppy and it is especially relevant to talk about this as the weather becomes colder and the darkness increases.

It is not easy for a puppy to control his bladder because it is *tiny*. They don't have much capacity, and the urge to relieve themselves is often immediate, and it can take them a while before they remember to tell us that they need to go, and even longer to learn how to hold it how until they have reached an appropriate toileting area. At this juncture, please consider just how long it takes to toilet train a young child.

Puppies are often taught to pee and poop on command, which is fine as long as we understand that puppies need our company as they are finding the perfect spot to toilet. Never leave a puppy on his own to "get on with things", because they feel very vulnerable and are likely to become fearful without us to support them. Additionally, it is important not to rush a puppy when teaching him to pee and poop on cue. I have yet to know a human that could pee on request!

But it is not only puppies that need to be considered. How often have you needed to pee when you have been out and walked along a line of toilet cubicles and checked two or three toilets before going back to the first one? Or you may have chosen one and then realised the door doesn't lock, or it there may be something else about it that you dislike, so the whole process has to start again? *Choosing a place to pee is important for us, so why would it not be the same for our dogs?*

Careful thought needs to be given before starting to use a cue to make your dog pee quickly. At best it can make a dog uncomfortable, at worst it can take away one of the most important times in a dog's day. Let your dog enjoy his rituals and allow him to ponder, sniff and take pleasure in deciding where to do his business.

Keep Up!

The other day I saw a post on a Facebook group that gave details of a dog friendly website where canine businesses could advertise their dog related services. I found the site and filled in all the relevant details as I am in the process of promoting my canine enrichment area as a place of interest for both dogs and their carers'.

The benefits of visiting an area which has specially been set up for dogs to explore, investigate, and move at leisure is becoming clearer and clearer to me since starting the venture.

Many dogs have visited since it was opened, including reactive and nervous dogs that are either fearful around other dogs, or are uneasy about a lot of noise and movement. For these dogs too much unpredictable sensory stimulus increases worry and anxiety. The site I had added the details to denied my request and turned it down. The reason for this? The answer was "the training area looks like it could be somewhat unsafe".

There is more to life with dogs than training.

I specifically gave the information that the area is designed as a place of sanctuary, and provides sensory adventure for dogs. It would be a bit lame to offer that and then present a flat area full of nothing more interesting than a few blades of grass.

How long is it going to be before websites that feature

places for dogs and owners to visit, and *make* their money from canine professionals, to understand that not all areas are for training purposes? As an added bonus many human visitors, especially those with anxious and newly rescued dogs have commented during their visits that it is one of the only times *they* can truly relax when they are out with their dogs. They able to shed their tensions and feel the serenity of the area seep into their own bones.

Education is an ever-increasing uphill struggle. Our dogs deserve areas to relax and unwind, just as we do.

Bugs for dogs?

Last week I visited a trade show which featured all kinds of pet related products for animals, but mostly features dog foods and treats.
I don't think I have ever seen so many vegan/ vegetarian foods for dogs in one place and there were also a few companies present that had formulated foods which replace animal protein (chicken, turkey etc) with bug-based foods such as meal worms

I am not totally on board with this, but that is my personal reaction, I know there is a lot of solid anecdotal evidence that says plant protein can fulfil the needs of dogs.

With this in mind I took some samples home for my dogs to try and they turned their noses up which is unusual. This makes me wonder if there will be many dogs that find the bug substitute truly palatable? There is no doubt a dog could exist and even thrive on a vegan diet, but would it be a diet that they would choose?

A Dog For All Seasons

1-2-1 time

Recently I responded to a question on social media -the question was about whether the person could walk 3 dogs together if she got another dog. I replied that I have 3 dogs but walk them all individually. There are many reasons why I do this - because I feel they enjoy some individual time, not just with me, but because it gives them time away from the others and have some alone time.

Some of that time is spent sniffing but each dog chooses to walk in a different way. One of my greyhounds is a "skipper" she bounces along but makes regular pauses to press her face into wedges of grass and sniffs around feathered grasses, and will then continue to press her face underneath them before changing to daintily sniffing the other bits of the plant where other dogs have peed.

One of my other dogs enjoys a bit of squirrel watching and can spend ages scanning the areas where we wander. She does this very politely and when we go to squirrel free areas, she is happy to potter around off lead. My third dog is always slightly worried, and doesn't much like other dogs so it is rare for him to totally relax when he is out, but he does love to run so we find quiet places where he can chase a few birds. or dash headlong around a field, or investigate a river.

This helps him to settle and find his own rhythm for the rest of the walk, which without fail ends up fairly slow as we inevitably have a stretch of road to travel along before reaching home.

If you have more than one dog do think about what each dog needs and whether individual walks might be worth providing from time to time so that they have agency and

choice.
Enrichment

Enrichment is so beneficial for dogs. We can make it enjoyable, but we can also mess things up for them. What enrichment is not about is luring dogs with food or dropping the odd puzzle onto the floor or scattering a few treats around. Our dogs deserve more than this and although puzzles are better than nothing, they can create frustration and should be given to our dogs after they have eaten. They should not be used by themselves to provide meals. Nothing creates frustration quicker than using puzzles as a means of feeding a hungry dog.

I think we can all identify with the concept of "hangry". If I went to a takeaway or restaurant and was asked to search for my food, it is unlikely I would stay Enrichment is not about compromising a dog, and more importantly it does not have to be about food. Enrichment is about movement, enjoyment, and encouraging dogs to use ALL of their senses, including the lesser known vestibular and proprioceptive senses as well as providing an outlet for natural behaviours .

Enrichment can help traumatised dogs and encourage relaxation and clear thought. If used correctly it can reduce stress levels, instill curiosity and is one of the best ways of helping an emotionally damaged dog to feel safe. It can encourage dogs to move in different patterns and to place their feet on areas, and walk on textures that they may normally shy away from. This helps create balance and a sense of wellbeing.

If dogs are able to think about specific placement of their feet and the freedom to navigate an area it has huge benefits. Movement prevents stiffness and helps us all to make good decisions therefore using areas of the brain which might otherwise not be called on during a routine day.

Think carefully about what you provide as enrichment for your dog, and not to buy into the huge pet market. There are things around us all that can enrich our dog's lives without putting money into the pockets of huge corporations such as utilising cardboard as rummage boxes, use loo roll tubes, pick up feathers during walks and rub cloths on trees and lampposts that dogs have visited to provide novel scents. These are of interest to dogs and combine items from nature which are all incredibly valuable to dogs.

Dressing up

Are you considering dressing your dog up for Halloween? Please think again. It seems to have become increasingly popular over the last 10 years or so. During Halloween and Christmas, it seems to be routine for dogs to be included when it comes to seasonal wear.

Dogs are not children, and neither are they here to provide us with entertainment but for many people dressing dogs up has become acceptable and even obligatory when it comes to celebrations. There is a point where a discussion is needed which informs dog carers that dressing their dogs up can be uncomfortable or even detrimental for their dogs.

Our dogs have evolved over many millions of years to become the species they are today. Without doubt they are tolerant of most things we force on them, but we need to become more aware of canine body language and how our own behaviour impinges on their wellbeing.

Dogs have- by nature- amazing coats which are functional, comfortable and generally well adapted to cope with fluctuations in temperature, providing we allow them to find areas that help them to regulate homeostasis. In the winter this may include being on our sofas or beds which provide warmth and safety. Our dog's skin (and fascia) is the largest organ in the body and their bodies need to be able to move without interference.

Their tactile sense is highly developed via sensors in the skin but loading more information onto the body via artificial layers is not necessarily enjoyable for dogs. Having said that there are of course exceptions for specific breeds where an extra layer can be of help with regulating temperature and can help provide relief in hot conditions, among these breeds are greyhounds and smaller breeds with less body fat and are likely to feel extremes of temperature. These breeds often appreciate a well fitted fleece coat or other properly designed layer when temperatures drop, increase, or when it is rains. Other than that, our dogs are amazingly prepared for varying weather conditions.

Having established that our dogs generally do well without our interference what are the impacts of dressing our dogs up for Halloween, Christmas and all the other random festivals that seem increasingly frequent? Certainly, in past and ancient history dogs were decked out with a bit of bling, mostly in the form of collars but these were often functional and worn to prevent injury. The bulky collars often seen in old paintings were used on dogs to provide protection during hunting but would not have compromised movement too much, and the ornate collars sported by dogs belonging to nobility and royalty would have not been too restrictive when worn. The use of clothing to amuse humans is a more recent trend.

Predictably social media, celebrities and social media influencers can be blamed for most of the popularity, as it seems they love using their own dogs to accessorise their own choice of clothing. It is about time that it is understood that dogs would not elect to be clothed by us and that they are likely to feel awkward and restricted while wearing most of the costumes we choose.

There is even a national "dress your dog up day", which should raise the issue of how ethical it is for these events to be promoted. People often become defensive if it is pointed out that their dog is not happy about being dressed up to look like a pumpkin or a "hot dog". It might even be considered that forcing a dog to wear clothing in order to keep him clean is also detrimental and can have an adverse effect.

Dogs do become dirty and choose to run, jump and roll in mud and in other unsavoury aromas but is this not one of the things we should expect? Often these behaviours are the result of being sprayed or shampooed with perfumed products which dogs find unbearable. We might love the smell of baby powder, coconut, honeysuckle or vanilla (and this is after just a quick internet search) but would a dog choose any one of these scents when he has a sense of smell 1.000 to 10,000 times more sensitive than our own?

Communication should be part of living with a dog, it is unacceptable for anyone to be oblivious of obvious discomfort or anxiety when it is exhibited by our dogs. The signs will include moving away or struggling as the clothing is put on, as are lip licking, yawning, freezing, whale eye, and turning away, but there are many more.

Look at the dog's facial expression and how he holds his body. Look at the way he moves and whether he moves less when he wears clothing. He may roll, or chew at the material or become immobile. None of these are signs that a dog is "enjoying" the experience. Negative associations can also be formed when dogs are cuddled by young children because they look cute. Children may be forgiven for behaving like this when they see dogs in costumes as they look more like toys, but this doesn't make it right or acceptable.

We also have to consider how the clothing is made. We are all familiar of being irritated by a label or badly sown seams in clothes we are wearing. We have the option of removing the offending article or cutting out a label, we can also choose the fabrics we wear and what quality they are -it is unlikely these facts are considered when dog costumes are made. Having done another quick search many dog costumes are mass produced by supermarkets and cheap to buy, which means the quality is low. This is what we subject our dogs to when we pick one out with the rest of our shopping. Money is the name of the game *not* the comfort of the dogs.

There is also another very important consideration, that of pain. Many people are in denial about the presence of pain when it comes to their dogs. Arthritic conditions are very common. Pain can be present in any breed or age of dog but often has to be pointed out to dog owners. Lack of sleep and general low- grade pain and stress can result in allodynia. Allodynia is defined as a pain resulting from a stimulus such as light touch which would not normally provoke pain. It is the mechanism that the body uses to protect itself during healing. Allodynia can also be the result of emotional trauma as well as physical problems.

In respect to dog costumes it means that a dog may experience severe reactions when wearing any clothing. This is without even touching the topic of sensory processing and what is going on around the dog when celebrations like Christmas are under way. When we combine these factors, it is not surprising that so many dogs are surrendered to rescue after Christmas due to "aggression".

Do we have really enough knowledge to insist that our dogs wear clothing however cute or endearing they look? Is our happiness more important than theirs or do we continue to learn more about our dogs so that we can become more empathetic and stop looking at their worlds through our eyes?

We have the power to either enhance the lives of our dogs or to carry on believing that our dogs actively enjoy being dressed up.

Enlightening

A conversation whilst walking with a couple of clients and their dogs lead to a discussion of which lights would be more appropriate to use when walking as the nights grow longer. Should lights be used on dog's harnesses or collar so that dogs are visible while walking in low light?

Some people favour flashing lights, but careful thought needs to be given before purchasing.

Reflective clothing or bands on harnesses or collars, wearing reflective clothing yourself, or collars or attachments that give out steady light are all helpful in illuminating the presence of dog and carer during darkness

There is no evidence that flashing lights are detrimental for dogs but nevertheless a dog's eyes are not geared up for lights that blink on and off.
When some research was done this was found

Do flashing lights affect dogs?
Dogs, are more than three times as sensitive to the type of flicker produced by LED lights than humans.

With this information in mind please consider how your dog experiences light and how best to make you both visible in low light. Dogs have better night vision than we do, so it doesn't make sense to attach something to their bodies that might have an adverse effect on their senses.

Grab the sun while you can!

Take your dog and a cup of something nice and a treat for your dog (my greyhound likes a rabbit's ear) and find a sunny sheltered place and enjoy 20 minutes relaxation.

- It will boost your health
- Increase the bond with your dog
- Reduce anxiety-for both of you

The birds are still singing, and the sun is still warm, so make the most of it.

My dog is terrified of fireworks-what can I do?

This section provides a programme to help reduce your dogs fear during firework season

The next few pages contain information about how to help firework phobic dogs. Some of the advice is general and will be of benefit for dogs which suffer from thunder storms too and many of the points raised can contribute to providing better lives for any dog.

While it is difficult to totally eliminate fear during this time, what this section aims to do is to help reduce fear which will make this time of year easier for both dogs and carers.

Part 1
The background to fear of fireworks

Autumn is the season many dog carers dread. This is because it is the run up to firework season. For some dogs this is of no consequence, but many thousands of dogs suffer every year as a consequence. Dogs are by no means the only ones to suffer, there are many other animals and humans that are negatively impacted. The more pressure we put on the bigger supermarkets and Government the better. With this in mind this section is about how to help your dog through this period. As firework season approaches think very carefully about the nature of fear, and why fireworks can create such profound anxiety in many dogs.

Dog carers tend to search for remedies that not only address the fear but will eliminate it. They start to search for ways that will arrest their dog's fears, but why does it happen? Fireworks generally start to become a problem as the nights become colder and darker and this can prompt an association in the mind of a dog.

It's amazing that many people marvel about their dog's ability to connect these transitions with the beginning of firework season. These changes can result in phobic dogs becoming reluctant to leave the sanctuary of their home. If dogs had no power of recollection the species would have died off many thousands of years ago and, therefore, would not have been able to evolve into the animals we now live with. Fireworks contain specific elements including bright flashes and loud dramatic booms and bangs. These impact far more on our dogs' senses than they do on ours, because our senses are far poorer.

This is one of the reasons that the noise of the fireworks has become louder over the years. People crave more sensationalism because they find it thrilling and this has prompted the manufacturers to create louder and more powerful fireworks. It is impossible trying to explain that these booms and reverberations are all a "a bit of fun", because deafening noises normally indicate something bad is going down. If we heard identical but unexpected noises, we would be just as concerned, and there is no doubt that this type of noise would startle and unsettle us too, particularly if we were already experiencing some degree of anxiety and stress.

If we heard these identical noises when relaxing they would be less likely to provoke such strong emotions. We might just look around for an explanation but without becoming too worried. We live in a pretty peaceful country, so we are not primed to expect bad things. Our bodies might still produce the chemicals we need to get us out of danger, but once we had realised what had caused them, and there was no cause for concern, we would quickly return to a relaxed state. If that same noise did turn out to signal danger and threaten our safety, we would either stand and face it, run, or even sometimes against our better judgment, our bodies might go into freeze mode. These are all automatic reactions, and they are built into our bodies and brains to keep us alive.

This is what we are up against when discussing what to do about the effect that fireworks have on our dogs. The first thing we need to make sure of is that we don't make things worse. Fireworks are unpredictable and the brightness and sound they create are not under our control, unless, of course, we are the ones that set them off.

This is something that resonates with our dogs, and the days leading up to firework season are critical in helping our dogs through what is frequently a very difficult period for many animals and people with serious mental illness like PTSD (Post traumatic stress disorder).

Part 2

The connection between noise and pain

September can be warm, if a little humid, so there are plenty of storms around which create panic in many dogs. The one good thing about storms is that they are generally over pretty quickly. This is predominantly of concern to those people with dogs that suffer from noise phobias. The question is how should we address these phobias of loud noises?

Firstly, there is a link between fear of noises and pain, so this is the obvious place to start when trying to understand any kind of sensitivity to noise especially firework phobias.

Why would sound have an impact on pain?

Think about the last time you were startled by a noise. Did your body tense as you jumped and took a deep breath in? It's likely you did because loud or disturbing noises alert the sympathetic system and prepare us to respond to immediate danger. That startle involves the body. Our bodies gear up in readiness for flight. If a body is in pain, it doesn't take a lot to associate a specific noise -thunder for example - with pain which can occur as the body tenses and readies itself for action.

This startle can set off an acute muscle spasm, which in turn can lead to a negative association with loud noises. This is why pain is often at the root of extreme fear of loud and unpredictable noises such as fireworks and thunder. The process of finding out exactly where the pain originates from and how to address it can be a long difficult process but it is worth initiating.

A vet may be unable to find pain because it's not an easy thing to pinpoint, particularly if a dog is worried about being examined. The most useful thing you can present your vet with, along with your dog, is a diary of all the changes you have noticed that deviate from your dog's normal behaviour, movement and routines. For example, if your dog never seemed to mind stepping on and off kerbs, but now takes a lot more time and care whilst negotiating them, is avoiding the stairs in your house, or is showing a reluctance to walk into a certain room, will all be of help to your vet in the search for a diagnosis and may indicate that these obstacles are too treacherous to navigate, due to pain being present in the dog's body.

If pain cannot be found do discuss medications to help decrease your dog's anxiety with your vet. The most current medication which seems to helping many dogs is Sileo. This needs advance planning because any medication you intend to use needs to be available for you to administer as you become aware that fireworks are likely to be let off.

Making sure the right steps are in place *before* they are needed is integral to helping your dog.

Part 3
Why posture is important when changing negative to positive

Early Autumn as we are discussing is the time when a plan is needed to help with firework phobia. It's no good worrying about the imminent approach of fireworks when the end of October is in sight.

Think about popular songs and sayings such as "smile and the world smiles with you", "smile though your heart is aching", and how many people participate in activities like laughter yoga because they enhance their mood. There are myriad examples of how smiling and laughter can change our outlook on life.

This is exactly the same for our dogs. This does not mean you need to play these songs need to anxious dogs or involve them in yoga classes. But it is worth discussing the connection between anxiety and stress, the way in which posture alters as fears accumulate which in turn influence demeanor. Posture can inform us of exactly how a dog feels and is how he is experiencing the world. The challenge is to reduce anxiety, boost confidence and enhance mood by encouraging a dog with anxiety to use his very well-developed senses. Inviting your dog to do a treat search, or some nose work in the garden is a good beginning and will engage the senses.

Activities which kick start curiosity, and the pleasure of exploring can initiate the release of serotonin among other beneficial hormones and create a "feel good" emotional state. The choices we offer our dogs are important. Dogs' patterns of movement are similar to our own in as much as they often perform the same movements day in and day out, unless we provide more diverse opportunities. Careful thought is needed about the kind of activities we offer so we can facilitate change by helping our dogs to perform different patterns of movement, and to ensure that they enjoy and become invested in activities that are fun. In short activities should be enjoyable but not *exciting*.

Dogs are already good at stretching as much as they need to-our role is to provide things of interest so they motivate a dog with poor posture into reaching for a nice bit of food, or to investigate a novel scent that may not normally be available. Movement is a game changer. As the body moves and the dog starts to enjoy the activities, the more fluid posture will become and will evolve for the better.

Any dog that starts to move in a way that feels good will start to repeat the pattern of movement and more importantly, it becomes unconscious and easy. As posture changes to a more natural and relaxed stance it also changes the state of the mind.

What kind of activities can we offer that will kick start this type of change?
Any area that has various elements dotted around can pique interest, an example of the places which can be of help are sensory gardens or enrichment areas, many are now being set up and some may be local to you and can provide lots of ideas. Different elements can intrigue even the most anxious dogs and provide motivation. But be clear that a dog must have the energy to explore and to climb on and off things, or to investigate things at their leisure.

Integration of the senses is a great healer and incredibly

beneficial when it comes to improving outlook. More importantly the dogs themselves must be allowed to decide how to negotiate any areas or objects and what is "just right" for them.

The things that can be used to achieve beneficial changes include different textures, such as leaves, grass, straw, shavings or earth. Pallets to climb on and off, tyres to step into and out of, logs and branches to look under and step over, inclines to negotiate and both indoor and outdoor areas can provide visual stimulation and will vary with the light and weather.

The changes in the seasons also provide interesting and novel experiences and can be made use of. People may dismiss enrichment areas or sensory gardens that have been created by professionals, but personal experience has shown only positivity for many dogs with confidence issues. This includes watching and monitoring how movement changes as the sessions progress.

The benefits include:

- A growth in confidence and independence
- Changes in posture and movement-tails relax and lift, expression is more open, and the steps become longer and more fluid
- Increased suppleness and mobility and freedom of movement

Elements of enrichment can be put together on a smaller scale in your garden or any quiet area either indoors or outdoors and can be utilised in the same way to facilitate posture, mood change, increased range of movement, suppleness and flexibility, which combine to lift mood and positivity. As you walk with your dog many of these elements can be included and can be sprinkled with little departures from the normal routine.

Take some different and varied treats to encourage your dog to sniff and explore by putting them in the bark of trees, use different textures to walk on, walk up, down and along grassy banks, step over logs, use gates instead of walking around obstacles, all fire the proprioceptive sensors. All of these can be found on many walks, and can be employed and used as a form of mood enhancing rehabilitation.

Movement is all important in the process of finding a solution to firework phobia. The saying "Curiosity conquers fear "is valuable and illustrates how these additions to your routine can form part of the jigsaw when tackling firework phobia.

Part 4

Put the balls away!

The link between the exercise and anxiety

If dogs spend their time running fast to catch balls for many hours a week, there is an impact on their physiology. When dogs run for the sheer fun of it, this is voluntary, but when they run to chase balls, they get caught up in an ever-escalating cascade of hormones. These hormones and neurotransmitters are primarily lifesavers and are ever ready. In emergency situations they serve to switch the flight/ fight/ freeze mechanisms on, which will prompt the body to take action or to shut down. These reactions are not under conscious control, as often there is no time for rational thought, but they are essential as they exist to preserve life.

These hormones are ready to be released in extreme situations, but if for some reason they are constantly present in the body, this creates unnecessary anxiety and can lead to chronic stress. If a dog is chronically stressed *and* hyperalert it is a recipe for disaster.

A firework phobic dog that has cortisol and regular injections of adrenaline into the body (via exercise of the wrong type) has a heavy burden to carry as his body is ever ready to respond to threats. One of the best ways of turning this situation around is to change the type of exercise the dog is getting. If a dog is perpetually running after balls and chasing around there is not enough time for the hormones and chemicals in the body to return to "normal" before the next session begins. This type of exercise causes dogs to be restless and it can appear to many carers that their dogs need more exercise in order to make them tired.

The biggest problem is that fast exercise involving balls is addictive to many dogs. Obsession is unhealthy and creates connections in the brain that cause dogs to make bad decisions and create permanent and often negative changes to the brain. Any activities create pathways in the brain and become well used through practice. It may be difficult to change the habit of taking a ball out for your dog but there are ways of reducing the reliance you or your dog may have.

This does not have to be done in one hit. If balls are thrown less often and instead are hidden in undergrowth or placed or rolled along the floor so the dog has to retrieve them improve a dog's relationship with balls can be improved. This about turn is incredibly beneficial and will help to reduce anxiety. If fast activities are reduced, it gives time for the stress chemicals in the body to reduce naturally resulting in the dog becoming less anxious and more able to cope with worries such as fireworks.

The other problem with dogs running after and jumping for balls is a physical issue. It has been shown that there is a strong connection between dogs chasing and catching balls with arthritic changes in the body, and as discussed earlier there is a correlation between pain and fear of loud noises.

When preparing your dog for the firework season, it is not prudent to continue to encourage activities that raise stress levels and contribute to a month of misery while fireworks are being let off.

Our dogs have few choices on many aspects of their lives they have to depend on us to make good choices for them. This is one of the easiest fixes you can include in a dog's routine and will promote and enhance your dog's life.

Suggestions for alternative exercise

All walks should include some running if your dog is happy off lead, but *must* include a warming up and cooling down period. If a dog arrives home panting and restless this indicates overstimulation which means a dog is both physically and mentally tired, and this will impact on rest and sleep.

- Warming up means at least 10 minutes walking/trotting before moving at faster speeds
- Cooling down should consist of enough time for a dog to stop panting and should include a period of sniffing
- Voluntary running exercises joints and keeps muscles functional, and some slow "moochy"

- walking, helps to cool the body down and reduce breathing and pulse rates
- weekly regular low- key meetings with a friendly dog to play and socialise should also be instituted

Altering exercise will make a huge difference to a firework phobic dog, but should become a permanent fixture rather than being put in as a fix before firework season.

Inevitably, there will be a period of change to allow both dog and carer to become less reliant on balls and to encourage the dog to practice natural behaviours. There is one more thing. Add good natural chews into your dog's day-there have been studies that say chewing is actually a form of exercise!

Part 5

Canine therapy

Many people can't quite see how a therapy would fit into a dog's life, but be assured that dogs can benefit from bodywork as much as people. Obviously, they can't do their research and make the call to book themselves a session, so we need to advocate for our dogs, and make decisions for them.

There is no better time than the first few weeks of September to think about booking some bodywork for your dog if he suffers from anxiety and worry around firework season, but don't dismiss it at other times of the year either. There are many therapies around but at this point we are going to discuss Bowen therapy as the author is an experienced practitioner.

How can Bowen help a dog with a phobia?

Firstly, no therapy is a cure all, but they can help to reduce stress and any pain that is present in the body. As the nights lengthen and dogs start to anticipate loud noises and flashes of light, Bowen can provide some relief.

- It is relaxing, and can address restrictions in the body.
- Can help address posture and gait abnormalities.
- Is gentle and only works on soft tissue. There is no manipulation of hard tissue which some dogs and people find a little harsh.

A full assessment is taken before any treatment. This is fed back to the carer and advice on exercise and how to reduce stress is given. It is always important to plan for 3 sessions which need to be fitted in before the loud bangs and crashes begin.

What is Bowen therapy?

The Bowen Technique is one of the lesser-known alternative therapies; this is because it has not been around for as long as more familiar therapies such as chiropractic work or osteopathy. Acupuncture dates back thousands of years and both massage and chiropractic work have been practised for hundreds of years.

Bowen has different roots altogether. It was born out of the work and research of Tom Bowen in Australia, and he founded a therapy that is quite remarkable. It differs from other forms of body work because it lets the brain translate the messages that are being given to the body because breaks are given during the treatment. The essence of Bowen is that it is subtle and non-manipulative. Bowen therapists work only on soft tissue and muscle, and use rolling movements made with fingers and thumbs and the treatment takes in the whole body. The pressure used is minimal, to be more precise this is never more than you could bear if you put your own finger onto your eyelid and pushed gently without it becoming uncomfortable. Tom Bowen discovered that the body didn't need a huge amount of pressure applied to it before the brain started to pick up on the messages. The other big difference between Bowen and other therapies is the presence of timed breaks during treatment. The breaks are one of the most important features of Bowen.

Pain and stiffness are the most common reasons to seek out Bowen. However, it not only addresses pain, but it can have a highly beneficial effect on emotional and long-term health. With regard to animals, this aspect is important, since we cannot know if what appears to be a physical problem may not in fact be linked to something far more complex, for instance in the case of stress.

The result of any treatments may appear to be subtle but by helping release tension and stress and assessing how the dog is coping it is often easy to see a positive result.

Part 6

Look after yourself!

Whilst discussing what affect fireworks can have on our dogs, we can't overlook the tension that is created by looking after a dog that is perpetually worried and hyperattentive to the environment, so don't forget yourself!

Looking after a dog that is severely distraught is a stressful experience, so while you are thinking about your dog and making sure you eliminate stressors, make sure that you are prepared too, because it is hard going. Bodywork for people can be of immense value to humans so book yourself in for a few sessions of pampering or take some time out.

Bowen was discussed in the previous section, and it's very possible you could receive Bowen alongside your dog, but of course there are other ways of giving yourself a bit of time out. If you don't have a way of defusing your stress this is a good time to explore how this can be put in place. This might be provided through socialising, going for a meal, taking a short break somewhere, or just having a long soak in the bath!

Our dogs need us, and it is a mistake to overlook the toll it will takes on personal health and wellbeing. Our dogs rely on our help and understanding, by neglecting yourself you might just run out of energy at a critical time.

Part 7

The connections between the gut and the brain

Did you know the gut is often referred to as the second brain? The gut microbiome is incredibly important when it comes to the wellbeing of our dogs. The gut manufactures more serotonin than the brain but is dependent on what is going on within the dogs' gut and there is a connection to what is being ingested. There is no one food that is more likely to provide a good microbiome so by providing your dog with a good, varied diet, which is well balanced, should help achieve healthy and varied bugs within the gut.

The importance of a healthy gut couldn't be more relevant if you have a firework phobic dog, because the gut needs to be able to produce the right balance of hormones and neurotransmitters. Without beneficial microbes in the gut, it's possible that we are missing out on a crucial part of helping to address the worry and stress. This is one time where good connections between the gut and brain are crucial in helping to reduce the effect of worry and anxiety. It is always a good idea to have some probiotics on hand, which are now widely available on the internet.

The value of probiotics may still be debatable, but many people take them to provide a boost for their mental health. While there is no solid evidence that probiotics can help there is certainly anecdotal support for using them to support the immune system and the helping the microbiome to flourish.

Part 8

Social connections

Dogs are a very social species and good solid social connections are integral for dogs at all times of year, but they become even more essential during stressful times such as firework season. This does not mean spending a few extra minutes with your dog everyday while you walk. This is about spending valuable time being "present" with your dog, so ditch your phone and laptop and make sure you are available to your dog.

Connection is important for dogs that are anticipating their world changing and it's also at this point that your dog is bound to appreciate any good dog friends too. If these are missing from your dog's life it is a good time to look around for suitable companions. These gaps can often be filled by joining a social walk. There are many to choose from including walks run by canine professionals or there are specific breed walks run by charities, rehoming centres, or groups. For example, there are many regular organised greyhound walks which are advertised on social media, and a search is likely to result in one near to where you live. The bonus of these walks is that they are normally on lead and if some dogs are off lead this is policed by the organisers.

Social walks involve sharing time and likeminded activities such as sniffing, treat searches and valuable calm social interactions and very often there is time at the end for the humans to have coffee, cake and a natter. There are no downsides to providing solid canine social connections for your dog

This is the end of the suggested programme that can be put in place as a preparation to firework night, but what of the actual night itself?

Firework night

Date night with your dog

The day that 5th November falls on will dictate how much of a problem it is likely to be, as will the weather. If it falls on a weeknight and the weather is wet this actually signifies that the "celebrations" are likely to last longer.
If it falls on a weekend it is just possible that the night of 5th November will be the worst night and the following days will be a little easier. This is part of the problem with this time of year, it is unpredictable and the only certainty is from the organised firework displays that occur in your local area.

Consider firework nights as date nights with your dog.

- In the weeks leading up to firework night keep exercise calm. Knock the agility on the head, you can resume at a later date. A tired dog that has escalating levels of adrenaline and stress hormones circulating in the blood is ill prepared to cope with the sheer unpredictability of fireworks- tiredness does not equal calmness

- Take your dog out early and make sure any exercise has been relaxing and enjoyable, and make sure all windows are closed and curtains are drawn to help damp any noise down
- Make your home is as snug and comfortable as possible. Select some favourite films or TV series and prepare to have these running at all times
- You may also simultaneously need to have the radio on, but make sure the programme you select does not have any breaks. It is on the silences that dogs become alert to the noises from outside, this is why a film or TV programme is unlikely to help. Your dog- for once- is going to appreciate a wall of sound.
- Tightly fitting wrap around coats for your dog may be of help, but make sure your dog is happy to wear one before you need it.
- Chamomile tea might be of some help, but if you do make some up there should be a bowl of regular water beside it
- White noise can prove helpful as can non stop music. There are some studies that show specific music is more acceptable to dogs but you may not be able to find a way of making sure there are no gaps
- Administer any medication from your vet in good time

- Make sure your dog has a choice of places to go. Don't close doors or prevent him going where he feels most comfortable. If you have followed the programme suggested earlier you may well find that your dog is happy to stay cuddled up against you even if he is still worried. It is almost impossible to eliminate all the fear your dogs feels but if he will curl up with you, so you can comfort him when needed you have done your dog a great service
- Cook something that smells glorious and tastes good. There is nothing more comforting than the smell of food cooking, but don't overload your dog with carbs. They have the same effect on dogs as they do on us. We can feel full and happy for a while but once digested a dog may well feel less than happy. Treat yourselves to a stew or something that is protein based which will leave all of you feeling full and happy.
- If you can drive to an area where there are no fireworks this is often really successful, or alternatively take a holiday with your dog in a secluded location. But do check the locality before you book as many small villages and even isolated areas often have community fireworks

Have they gone?

The aftermath of the fireworks

After the fireworks have subsided think very carefully about what is planned in the days and weeks after. Even if your dog appears to have sailed through the firework frenzy, it is just as well to keep a careful watch and make sure you respond positively to any changes that occur during this time.

Very anxious dogs will have extremely sore muscles and bodies from being tense for hours on end, and they are likely to ache and feel stiff which will have the effect of making them feel under the weather. The lesser-known sense of interception can't be seen from the outside, but the aftermath may result in your dog feeling extremely compromised

It is also likely that firework phobic dogs will have moved into a chronic stress mode so their behaviour may be very odd. This may include refusing food, being hyperalert and over reactive to even the most "normal" sounds. This complete assault on the sensory world of our dogs is not something that we are able to share, although many dog carers that have been trying to look after their poor bemused dogs will be feeling weary and worn out too.

Loud bangs and vibrations may have also affected and upset your dogs vestibular system and messed with their normal view of the world. If changes are detected in your dog's behaviour, please be kind. Many carers are so focused on what happens *during* the fireworks that they forget about what might occur after the event. Preparations for supporting dogs may also need to be planned in advance for Christmas and New Year celebrations.

Walks should be slower than normal as adrenaline and cortisol will be released quickly into the body if there is cause for alarm. Tasty food, and good quality chews and treats can help ease some of the worry and anxiety. If your dog likes bodywork then offer some to him, or if your dog already has regular bodywork then ask the therapist for an appointment. But now is *not* a good time to introduce something novel into a firework phobic dog's life. It is not a good time to gain a dog's consent to bodywork if triggers have been present in his life. Instead carry on with any activities your dog finds enjoyable, and which have been successful over the worst nights, for example calming music, tasty chews, and continue to walk only in broad daylight. Do *not* return to walking at dusk or at night, as this will only alarm your dog unnecessarily and *do* encourage rest and sleep and provide enrichment and quiet proprioception activities.

Dogs are able to predict bad things, just as we are, and this leads to negative associations, these things don't need to be part of your dog's life, so take care of your dog and nurture him after the fireworks have ceased

Beach time!
Despite the problems that arrive with the autumn there is a huge benefit for dog sas many beaches that dogs are banned from all summer now changes. So, the small things need to be celebrated along with the negatives.
There is nothing better than driving to a deserted windswept beach that belongs to you and your dog.
You may even get some half decent weather where you some fish and chips or an ice cream can be shared with your dog.

A Dog For All Seasons

There is no danger of heat stroke and journeys to the beach are always so much easier in the cooler weather

Enjoy!

A Dog For All Seasons

WINTER

Winter as with all the other seasons provides a multitude of different experiences for a dog, the weather gets colder, the ground becomes softer and muddy with lots of puddles that many dogs adore. If it is cold enough for them to freeze some dogs delight in trying to eat the ice.
It is darker, and daylight is limited and this all combines to have an effect on our dogs. But most of all winter can be difficult. Christmas is a time for family but there are reasons why so many dogs end up in rescue directly after Christmas. People forget that dogs need care and consideration throughout busy times, and the needs of a dog should not drop down the list during hectic times of year. The build up to Christmas and New Year is unpredictable for our dogs and they can't be expected to adjust to the mood or moderate how they feel when there is a lot going on around them.

   Winter is a time when sensory overload becomes a problem and this is referred to and discussed throughout this section.
Fortunately, winter is not all about Christmas but our attention does turn to food and warmth

"Such short little lives our pets have to spend with us, and they spend most of it waiting for us to come home each day." John Grogan

A Dog For All Seasons

Routine winter checks

The winter creates many changes and it is worth discussing at this point in the year because this creates disruptions in routine
A routine should not be about making your dog busy or creating a non stop social diary for him. Instead, it should include a huge dollop of checking in with our dogs, not in an intrusive way but rather with the odd glance such as we may give our friends when we meet them.

Some of the checks include watching that they are eating with the normal relish, (don't forget that your dog may appreciate you being around when eating because after all, it is a social activity and we humans often prefer eating in company).
The other benefit of this is to observe exactly how your dog is eating, whether he seems comfortable or whether he is avoiding eating specific foods which are normally devoured. Many dogs have bad teeth or even discomfort in the hard working joint at the top of the jaw which may prevent a dog chewing his food thoroughly. Ask yourself if any habits seem to be changing. For instance, one of my greyhounds always has a huge stretch before she goes out for her first pee in the morning, this stretch takes time and it ripples along her entire body and this pandiculation tells me all is well in her world.
This is not an extensive list but these simple pointers will help you keep track

- If your dog is as interested as normal especially when he is outside, and is his poop normal?

- Is your dog shedding hair-if so more or less than normal? All dogs shed hair but the amount is specific to each individual dog, and can signal changes in health or an increase in levels of stress. This is worth monitoring in a centrally heated environment -scurf in a coat can denote stress
- Have sleeping patterns altered?
- Is your dog interacting with you and your family as normal?

Routines are not always about what we do *with* our dogs, but more about observing them so we can allow our dogs to give *us* information.

Winter warmers

Winter is a time when we think of curling up in a cosy warm house with candles flickering, but fragranced candles are one of the luxuries we need to forgo if we have dogs. Closed doors and scented candles are not a good match when we live with dogs

This is why we need knowledge of the dogs' ethogram and physiology. Although it is becoming more widely known that dogs have to sniff and need to use their powerful sense of smell to remain balanced and happy, many people are ignorant of just how sensitive and highly developed the olfactory sense is.

These days I can't stand the smell of people walking past me if they have doused themselves in buckets of highly scented perfume or shower gel, and my sense of smell is nowhere as finely tuned as that of a dogs'.

I have often wondered and speculated on what it would be like to be a dog. What if we had the gift of being in our dogs' heads for 5 minutes? This would be just enough time to understand just how intense their sense of smell is. Actually, those 5 minutes may well be both incredibly interesting and horrifying because we would have the experience of just how highly developed their senses are, especially the olfactory sense.

This is why we should consider *all* the fragrances that we use in our houses and cars. Most of them are unnecessary and we have been led to believe by adverts on the TV and radio that our dogs give off such a pungent stink that synthetic perfumes need to be used to mask the smell. If your dog's coat or any area of his body does smell, please make an appointment to see the vet because this is not normal and can be a symptom of disease or an allergy. It is also a problem that many dog carers do not connect the link between chemical smells of candles, plug ins, carpet cleaners, bleaches and myriad other scents with the many behavioural problems that are reported. Artificial scents can create an overwhelming assault on a dogs' olfactory system.

Just consider a smell you can't tolerate and imagine that magnified by 1,000 times what impact would this have if you were unable to leave the area? With this in mind please leave the fragranced candles in the shop for people without dogs to purchase.

If your dog has suddenly developed allergies, the first step is to think carefully about whether your dog has any contact with fragranced products in your house, and do be prepared to find more natural or alternative dog friendly products. If your dog has continuing issues do make an appointment to visit your vet.

If you really are passionate about fragrances then confine

their use to well-ventilated areas where your dog has the choice to leave, but better still learn to live without them.

Solitary confinement

It is clear there is a huge disconnect between what people want and what dogs need. There is no point in bringing a dog into your home and thinking that your life won't change, because it will.

If you take on a dog book some time off and plan to spend it with him. Any newly rehomed dog needs support and help to adjust to a new environment, and this is why a busy holiday period such as Christmas is the very worst time to rehome a dog or take a puppy home. The other thing about hectic holiday periods is that sooner or later they finish and everyone has to return to work or school and a dog then has to readjust to being alone in a very quiet house.

Dogs rarely feel secure enough to be left alone for hours at a time until they feel safe and secure and both a bond and a routine has been established. Safety and security are essential to good mental and physical health for anyone including dogs. There are no quick fixes when preparing a dog to be left home alone, and there are far too many anecdotes about how to complete this training as fast as possible, if indeed it is "training" that is needed.

Never separate your dog from your company with the aim of preparing them for being on their own. Stories that circulate in the park which are freely offered by other dog owners should be taken with a pinch of salt. Confining dogs to specific rooms and isolating them from your company while you are at home will not stop them feeling scared and vulnerable and will not prevent "over attachment" There is little danger of separation anxiety if we help dogs build their confidence and we provide much needed company during the first few weeks, but there is a danger of creating insecure and unstable attachments if a dog is isolated and prevented from seeking out our company.

Ask yourself this-how would you feel if someone locked you in a room and you could hear them moving around, chatting and having dinner? It would be creepy, unsettling and would this help you to establish more confidence and more self- esteem? It is doubtful. Being in a house that is unfamiliar with is fraught with enough difficulties, without forcing dogs to be alone in the name of training.

Anxiety and stress levels will increase and often the results are vocalising, urinating or chewing as a result of fear and stress. These are cries for help.

Give a new dog your time and company, because this is what is needed to build confidence and a sense of security. Without our help they fail.

It's just a dog

Yesterday I was sitting with my very elderly mother in a cafe, her mental and physical halth is rapidly declining, so I was thinking about whether she was enjoying our visit. I like this particular cafe, my favourite table has really comfortable chairs, and I can stare out of the window and watch everyone going past. I realised while I was sitting that I could hear music, this surprised me as I had not noticed it before.

As I was pondering, I was also thinking back to a course

A Dog For All Seasons

I took a while back which needed serious consideration because it was about how dogs experienced the world and sensory integration difficulties. During one of these sessions the subject of noise, and the general hubub of people talking was being discussed, as you might find in a pub or a cafe, some of us that were attending the course understood the experience of finding these situations difficult, in particular being unable to carry out conversations with a single person in a distracting and noisy environment.

My thoughts carried on meandering. In my twenties I used to hate going to busy pubs because quite frankly I could never hear a thing anyone said, I thought this was a personal thing that was specific to me. Obviously, this is not true, but nobody else seemed to suffer with this at that point in my life. That led me to another thought about how this affects dogs, in particular, dog classes and social events such as Christmas where the family home is often filled with unexpected noise and activity.

This degree of discomfort which sometimes leads to bewilderment is why I no longer hold indoor classes for dogs, I have found that dogs are more comfortable outside and natural environments are more likely to put them at ease- as long as the right area is chosen. The outdoors offers room, and prevents voices echoing and being amplified, and if a dog is overwhelmed the carer can take them away for a while.

Returning to the problems of indoor classes, they are noisy, the halls are often packed, and someone recently told me there were 20-25 dogs in a class she attended. Her own dog lacks confidence and she said that her dog would often bark during the entire class. If she asked for advice, she was told to throw treats down.

How are dogs supposed to learn in that kind of environment?

If they like me had trouble "hearing" the cues among the general chatter and the requests that were being issued by the trainers, then quite frankly it is amazing our dogs are as good as they are (and this is just one of the minor problems in this situation). These types of indoor classes are still pretty standard fare locally and people won't hear a word said against them.

Do our dogs deal with sensory input differently to us? No, they don't, and yes, they *are* like us. We need to stop putting them in situations that they can't cope with and more pertinently these problems largely go unrecognised. Training should no longer uniformly consist of large halls that echo with the sound of excitement, and the smell of adrenaline that exists when many dogs are confined in an indoor area. Our dogs rely on us to identify these situations and we need the strength of mind to leave if we know they are stressed.

If we are not prepared to advocate for our dogs we have to accept that dogs will have difficulty with self- regulation, and this to the misinformed looks a lot like disobedience.

The more we talk about sensory overload and the impact it has on the welfare of our dogs the better.

Food for thought.

What did your dog eat today and how many different ingredients did he consume? It is likely that your dog had far less variation than you ate yourself. We have huge choices available and if we open the fridge and see nothing that appeals to us, we can go to a shop, café or restaurant.

Science repeatedly tells us that if our dogs had free choice, they would choose at least 50 different food types on a frequent basis

Despite the current and increasing popularity of vegan diets for dogs 65% of what a dog would choose would derive from an animal origin. We need to remember that dogs love different textures and flavours, and despite the adverts and the recommendations that proclaim how well a brand has been researched and provides all the optimum requirements, be prepared to accept that this may not meet a dogs need for variety, or texture.

Worms?

Do dogs need worming as regularly as we are constantly being told? We may worm religiously as advised but we don't actually know if they are carrying significant worm burdens or which worms are more predominant

This leads to many people worming their dogs to be on the "safe side", but there is a way of knowing for certain whether your dog has parasites, and can inform you of which types and if the worm burden is significant. Screening is better than administering tablets because it can provide an early warning system plus providing a much broader knowledge and insight into the health of your dog.

See the appendix for a link to a website that offers worm counts.

Fascial changes.

There are many things we need to monitor if we have dogs and one of the early warning systems is your dog's skin and fascia. Coats can look shiny and healthy but this is not the entire story, we also have to look at the texture of the hair and how their coats sit on their bodies. The skin should lie flat over the body and move as easily as if your dog was wearing a light cloth. Fascia is the technical name for the skin and hair that covers the dogs' body and it should appear unruffled and smooth.

Fascia is important as it provides us with a picture of what is going on underneath the skin. For example- ruffled areas that appear to stick up indicate muscle tension and spasms at a deeper level and the coat itself can mask problems which is why we need to look and learn to run our hands over our dogs with more than just a cursory touch.

Behaviour changes can be very subtle and can prevent us from looking more carefully, and of course dogs are pre-programmed not to exhibit pain. The forelimbs and areas of our dogs' backs and hips can suffer trauma and injury which we may have no knowledge of. One of the giveaways is dislike of a harness, especially if this is a recent change, or you may observe that your dog is unhappy when asked to wear a coat during the winter months. It is easy to overlook a dogs' unease if you use the same equipment on an everyday basis, but if your dog starts to shy away or lie down as you prepare for a walk there is something amiss.

All behaviour means something. It may be easy to overlook a slight resistance when putting a harness, collar or coat on your dog, or a sudden reluctance to get into the car, so identifying changes is crucial. Any deviation in the hair pattern or obvious twitches in a specific area when skin is touched are indictive of areas of discomfort.

Most dogs' coats vary throughout the seasons and they may need to wear layers during colder temperatures, so don't neglect the fascia. If you run your hands carefully over your dog you may detect areas of heat which signify "hot spots", these too indicate areas where pain and discomfort is present.

Pain in specific areas is never isolated in one area but seeps into other places in the body and can create anxiety when walking even to the point of reactivity. If a dog does not want to be touched, he can become defensive when other dogs approach, even if previously there have been no problems interacting with other dogs. Subtle changes that may initially appear to be trivial to us do not mean that restriction and stiffness is not present. The skin, fascia and coat of your dog act as an early warning system and by design should encourage and enhance mobility.

If pain is present fascia will tighten like clingfilm resulting in significant restriction and discomfort.

Sit!

Is sitting at a curb really necessary?
Dog carers rarely question why it is so important for their dogs to sit quietly at the curb while traffic screams past them. It is also rare for people to contemplate that the very act of sitting on a cold wet or frozen curb might be uncomfortable for a dog. This is especially pertinent in winter.

For many dogs including sighthounds sitting doesn't come naturally. Of course, they can sit but it is neither comfortable or easy to sustain. As a dog sits, he is employing powerful muscles which are activated as he performs the movement, this is why so many dogs fidget and will jump out of a sit as soon as they are released. Sitting to attention is neither a calming activity or one which dogs would choose to perform before they cross a road.

This doesn't mean a dog should rush across a road, it is just as easy to teach a stand before crossing, and it is far more comfortable during cold weather. This also applies to hot weather as concrete heats up rapidly, but in any case, dogs should not be exposed to excessive heat. There are other valid reasons why dogs should not constantly be asked to sit. These include the presence of injury, arthritic conditions, cruciate problems, and muscle atrophy. Certainly, young puppies should be exempted from constantly being asked to sit, because their skeletal and muscular systems are rapidly developing, and therefore easily damaged.

There are multiple things that we ask of our dogs without really thinking if they are necessary because we have been told they promote "good behaviour". This is frequently untrue, and it is time that we re-thought the value of many "obedience" exercises that we were once told were essential.

If a dog automatically sits in specific places, this is probably because we have had an input in this, but replacing stand for sit is a good alternative and it is a small price to pay when it comes to canine wellbeing.

Gut feelings

Have you ever had butterflies in your stomach? What about a gut wrenching experience, or have you been in a situation that made you feel sick? It is likely that we can all identify with these feelings but what does this have to do with our dogs?

The reason it is as pertinent to our dogs, as ourselves, is because we have a lot in common, and share the same kind of connection between the gut and the brain. Your dog's diet has a profound effect on his brain, in fact the gut is often referred to as the second brain. This knowledge of the gut and brain connection is not new. Hippocrates is quoted as saying "all diseases begin in the gut". How is it in these supposedly advanced times that the gut is often overlooked when we are seeking answers not just for diseases, but if behaviour change has occurred? The gut and brain are linked by the vagus nerve. The word vagus is Latin for wandering, as that is exactly what it does. The vagus nerve is the tenth cranial nerve but rather more importantly its travels take it from the brain stem to the colon and because of this it has an important role in connecting the gut- brain axis.

This gut- brain axis transforms information via the vagus nerve from food to feelings, which is pretty extraordinary. It also interfaces with the parasympathetic control not only the digestive tract but the heart and lungs. The brain itself uses the vagus nerve to communicate fight or flight messages to the body. (Just a quick reminder here about the damage that can be sustained if a dog is walked on a collar and lead, especially if corrections are given via the lead directly onto the neck when the dog pulls. The position of a collar ensures that it is entirely possible to cause direct damage to the neck and in particular the vagus nerve).

It has been found that the gut is far more influential than

the brain. Rather than the brain controlling and influencing the gut, as might be assumed, it is the gut that has the ability to function on its own through the enteric nervous system. The ENS is embedded within the gut and actually produces more neurotransmitters than the brain and controls production of many neurotransmitters including serotonin and dopamine therefore influencing the brain far more than the brain influences the gut, and more significantly it affects how we feel (and how our dogs feel) day in and day out. This explains why our emotions, brain and gut are able to affect our moods and wellbeing.

Recent research has linked depression, Pakinsons, IBS, autism and anxiety in humans to problems originating within the gut brain axis. What does this amazing part of our dog's body need to thrive? And more importantly why does it have such a profound effect on behaviour?

This is where it is necessary to talk about the microbiome. Within the gut are trillions of bacteria, they are made up of both good (or friendly bacteria) and bad strains; when good health is present the good bacteria outnumber the bad and are supported by a nutrient rich environment. Only when the balance gets tipped in the wrong direction, for example through stress or bad diet, do things start to go wrong. The GI tract is dependent on a good diet to be able to absorb energy and nutrients, if this does not happen negative changes start to take place within the gut. This is often what is referred to as leaky gut. Leaky gut is caused by gut permeability, which allows pathogenic bacteria and toxins to spread throughout the (dog's) body. Undigested food, toxins and pathogens in normal circumstances would not be able to breach the gut wall, but in this instance, they can escape into the body causing an inflammatory response. This also adversely affects the immune system which is closely tied to the gut brain axis.

This reaction can cause unavoidable problems within the dog's body. Not only does the gut suffer but it is also possible that toxins may enter the brain via the blood brain barrier. This is why a seemingly distant problem in the gut can have such a huge impact on the behaviour of your dog.

Earlier we discussed the fact that dopamine and serotonin are manufactured in the gut. These are not the only neurotransmitters/ hormones that are produced by the microbiome, but they are possibly the most familiar to the majority of us. Neurotransmitters have a profound effect on behaviour, therefore behaviour is impacted if the gut microbiome is disturbed. Without the correct "building blocks" which combine to manufacture them, the entire body suffers and creates behaviour change. It is hard to define exactly how an individual neurotransmitter works and what each one does, as there are so many connections within the brain and body; but it is possible to highlight a few of the reasons they are so important.

Seratonin, for example, is made from tryptophan which many people will associate with feeling peaceful and sleepy after a large Christmas dinner, but of course it is far more complex than that. As many people will know is often referred to as the happiness chemical. It affects mood, helps control levels of aggression, helps with temperature control and has links to appetite by telling us when we are full, but it is best known for elevating mood. Similarly, dopamine is very complex but it is associated with desire and reward. It also helps us to learn and focus by speeding up our reflexes, and has connections to movement. The microbiome also produces GABA another neurotransmitter that many people may be familiar with which itself has a huge range of implications and can has a huge influence throughout the body but is mainly associated with increased relaxation, reducing stress, alleviation of pain and helps to boost sleep.

The microbiome itself also has an impact on sleep, and as we all know it is important for dogs to receive around 14 hours of sleep a day. If this is not achieved the result is sleep deprivation. Dogs cannot "catch up" on lost sleep any more than we are able to, it needs to be a regular feature of our dog's days, if not then changes take place within the brain which alter learning and how memories are processed.

You may conclude from this that if specific components are added to a dog's diet they will help produce the correct balance, but of course it is not that easy. You can help by providing a good diet, but the entire subject is complex and still being researched. Also be aware that supplements will not always produce the wonderful results they may claim to help with.

You can monitor all aspects of your dog's health and behaviour to get a snapshot of how things are within his body. Checking your dog's skin, energy levels, and what comes out of his body in the form of faeces (in particular) will go a way to indicating how your dog is feeling. Be careful in particular of foul smelling faeces which often indicate a poor diet, a balanced diet will produce stools that have a slightly sweet smell.

There is one other facet to consider. Puppies that are born naturally have a huge head start (literally!) on those delivered via caesarean section and many breeds now need veterinary intervention to help them give birth because selective breeding for specific traits (such as short faces which affects the shape of the pelvis) have denied many breeds the ability to deliver puppies by normal vaginal birth. When a puppy is delivered naturally, they receive a huge dollop of crucial bacteria as they pass through the birth canal. If puppies are born via caesarean section, they miss out on these crucial bugs and microbes that they would otherwise receive as they are born.

The importance continues and accompanies a dog through his life and is why we cannot overlook how the gut affects and contributes to behaviour problems. There are many events which can adversely affect the microbiome and much that we don't yet understand but certainly stress, lack of sleep, uncertainty and inadequate food can lead to toxic changes and proliferation of toxins within the gut that kill off good bacteria and set off reactions which cause detrimental effects to behaviour and mood.

This second brain needs to be as well tended and looked after as the rest of the dog's body- which is another reason why you might want to lecture visitors about slipping your dog inappropriate rich food over Christmas!

Cold and attachment

It is cold, and there is a huge urge to walk fast and leave your dog behind to sniff if he is off lead.
This impulse to hurry becomes amplified if a dog is on lead, as you become increasingly cold while your dog spends ages investigating a bit of grass from all angles and taking deep satisfying sniffs.

We mostly understand that our dogs need this time to process the outside world and to have the freedom to investigate, but what if a dog is off lead, and owners lose patience and walk away? Sometimes people are even encouraged to do this with puppies in order to ensure that the recall is securely trained. Come when called or I leave you! Neither of these scenarios are good for dogs because it destroys trust and the process of building a bond can be damaged.

Attachment theory is at the core of establishing confidence and eliminating anxiety with dogs of any age and social buffering is important when it comes to ensuring that our dogs feel safe.

It is one of those important things that needs to be considered when we share our lives with a dog. If we are unable to understand that we need to provide safety and security and need to be dependable then our dogs are likely to become anxious and lose confidence. For many people this may seem a bit far- fetched but we have to face the facts, if we take a dog into our lives the best gift we can give is empathy. Quality of life is vitally important for our dogs and providing a half- life that suits us will not compensate for what our dogs lose.

It may sound a bit of a leap to talk about walking away from your dog if you are cold, but if we take our responsibilities seriously, we cannot disappear over the horizon or hide in the undergrowth in order to speed our dogs up in order to get home faster.

If your dog starts to develop anxiety when you leave the house or is generally becoming more anxious, then consider everything that you do including the possibility that your own demands may be at the root of the problem.

Wait as your dog explores and don't trick him into being hyper attentive on walks by hiding or walking away because trust will slowly deteriorate.

Is your dog "hypermobile"?

It can be really difficult to diagnose difficulties that a dog is having within his body as they may not be at all obvious. This is the case with hypermobility. Hypermobility is the term used to describe joints that flex beyond the normal range of movement. Joint hypermobility is common in the general human population. It may be present in just a few joints or it may affect the entire body.

If we, as humans, suffer from this we can at least relate our feelings and explain the problems we are having but this is hard to pinpoint with animals. Mobility, suppleness and big movement is almost as highly prized in dogs as it is in horses, and it is an obsession with many horse breeders, but some have not learnt to link the big movement that is so highly prized with balance issues and anxiety.

Dogs with hypermobility can't tell us how difficult it is for them to move even if the constant feedback from their bodies tells them how unstable they feel. If they suffer from unstable joints the ground underneath their feet must feel like ice. This can only be distressing and painful. I often wonder whether this is why my greyhounds find it so hard to walk on pebbly beaches, in fact I no longer ask them to do this because it is so obviously distressing. Instead, we walk on sand or stay on the seafront promenade.

This *could* signal that my greyhounds have unstable and hypermobile joints but I have no proof, so it remains something that needs to be monitored. Hypermobility may also indicate problems such as hip dysplasia. The hip joint can be so loose that a dog or puppy feels like he is constantly walking on stilts, and of course it is extremely painful.

Before dismissing a dogs' anxiety when out walking, do think about what he may be experiencing within his body. Anxiety can be triggered by the environment because traction and stability is not present but is replaced by the feeling of walking on marbles. Freezing is a common occurrence in newly rehomed greyhounds, not only because they are unused to so many things happening around them, but it might be worth speculating that it could be caused by walking on surfaces which are unfamiliar and which they perceive as unstable.

Without knowing for certain it is a consequence of hypermobility it can certainly be something to ponder on and work around in the early days of a greyhound going home

Monitoring how our dogs are responding to any environment we put them in is incredibly important. We need to remain present and mindful and ask questions that are not always easy to answer.

Quick fixes

How often have we heard or used the phrase "I wish I knew then what I know now".

It is a sad expression but it can be positive too. We can't change what went before or erase what may have happened in the past of a rescue dog, but we can use what we have learnt, continue to improve on our knowledge and make things better for the dogs we now have in our lives.

I often wonder how people attain the knowledge they do, either good or bad, and how people "choose a path" with their dogs?

There is still a huge amount of bad information in circulation about how to handle dogs and how they are likely to be "dominant". Dominance theory has been disproved time and time and yet many people steadfastly adhere to its principals, causing distress and anxiety to the dogs they live with. Cruel methods and aversives have no place in the lives of our dogs, especially if they have been advocated by someone who calls themselves a canine professional.

Dogs are not self- seeking or pushing to take over our homes, they just want to feel comfortable and safe, and this is what motivates many humans too, so why do so many people advocate methods that make dogs lives so miserable? A tired, stressed and anxious dog will often react by being defensive and this can kick start aggression, we would be likely to react in an identical way if someone was being cruel or unfair to us. Making the lives of our dogs comfortable should be our goal.

After many years of studying and working with dogs and horses, and doing my utmost to give the best advice and information, there are still people that dislike what they feel are "fluffy" answers. Learning can be challenging, and it can take a lot to admit that facts you once adhered to are wrong and are causing harm

If you seek advice or help with your dog, please do examine your priorities and think about how you would like your dogs' life to be. Carefree and happy? Or managed and stressful? Sometimes there is no neutrality. Read carefully what trainers and behaviourists post on their social media or blogs, who they associate with, and look at how they respond to their own dogs.

Once it is understood that problems are unlikely to be solved quickly, especially if they have developed over a long period of time, this is a good source of where to look for someone that you are happy to work alongside.
Long live people who seek out the best for their dogs and don't fall for obvious sensationalism.

Let sleeping dogs lie.

Winter tells our bodies to sleep. What did you feel like when you woke up this morning? Would you have liked to have turned over and gone back to sleep, or was it easy to leave the comfort of bed to go looking for a shower or breakfast? A deficiency in sleep makes itself known to us from the moment we open our eyes in the morning. Sleep is essential and amazingly complex. Without it we would die, but way before this critical point, it would become increasingly difficult to perform the easiest of tasks, and eventually we would suffer from hallucinations and death.

Sleep has recently been the subject of much research. It is a common belief that it is possible to catch up on lost sleep, but unfortunately this is not true, and the resulting effects of sleep deprivation can have drastic effects on health, after only one sleepless night. Not only do we suffer when we lose sleep but so do our dogs.

I often ask owners how much sleep they think their dogs need, and they are often wrong. Adult dogs need in the region of 14 hours of sleep a day, with puppies and larger dogs needing as much as 18 hours a day. Although dogs don't destroy the quality of their sleep as we do, by drinking caffeine, taking transatlantic flights or constantly staying up late to watch a favourite film, they can and do suffer from other problems that affect their ability to sleep, some of which are imposed on them by the humans they live with. Even for our dogs there is a strong link between wellbeing (both physical and mental) and sleep.

Sleep is an inelastic activity, it is not negotiable, but there are differences between human and canine sleep. Humans are *monophasic* which means that we generally take all our sleep in one go, while our dogs are *polyphasic* which indicates that they sleep for shorter periods but at many different points throughout a 24 hour period. Both slow wave sleep (the sleep of the brain) and REM sleep (the sleep of the body which paralyses the postural muscles) are necessary for dogs and humans alike, but a dogs' ability to reach REM sleep is significantly faster. A normal sleep pattern for a dog is to sleep, wake up, have a stretch, find a more comfortable position and then go back to sleep. This regular shift between sleep and wakefulness does not affect the quality or quantity of sleep and is a normal part of a dogs' life.

Another fact to remember is that dogs are predominantly nocturnal, this can be proved by looking at the evolution of the dog. Wild canids and wolves evolved to hunt in low light conditions at dawn and dusk, where there was no need to differentiate between bright colours, as everything takes on a grey hue during these parts of the day. Even though this is a now distant memory, dogs still only see muted colours. Red for instance, is not on the dogs' colour spectrum. Although our domestic dogs are much removed from this distant past, nocturnal wakefulness can be observed in some situations, for instance in young puppies. They can often be up and raring to go just as the humans in the family are winding down and preparing for a night's sleep. There are many other reasons for this scenario too, this but the genetic memory still exists.

Despite the basic differences between sleep patterns of dog and humans, sleep is one of the things that we cannot overlook when it comes to the wellbeing of our dogs. Sleep is integral for many reasons including helping to consolidate memories, promotion of healing and helping to repair and restore the immune system. It has an effect on cognitive abilities and allows the brain to play out possible outcomes and prepares us for future events. It also helps to maintain a flourishing microbiome. Without the right amount of sleep the body cannot repair itself as easily and it makes our ability to learn much harder.

Nobody, either dog or human, can retain facts or new skills without the correct amount of rest. Other downsides of decreased sleep are the inability to regulate body temperature, less interest in body care and a tendency to over reactivity. Noises and weird shapes become scary, and "spookiness" is not uncommon. Because we control so much of our dogs lives we need to be especially tuned into how to enhance our dogs sleep. This needs knowledge of what can prevent good sleep as well as methods of promoting it.

<u>What prevents dogs getting the right amount of sleep?</u>

One of the most common reasons is over stimulation. Our dogs usually enjoy getting out and about as much as we do, but there are limits to how much a dog can cope with before he becomes frustrated and tired. It is common for puppies to jump up, grab the lead and refuse to carry on walking when they begin to tire.

This is why it is so important to have a basic understanding of canine communication and the canine ethogram. There are only a few ways that our dogs can try to tell us that they are tired and need to return home. We on the other hand are conditioned to believe that dogs need a vast amount of exercise and stimulation every day. This is certainly not true for most dogs, and they are just as likely to suffer from aching muscles and fatigue as we are, especially young dogs under a year old. If encouraged to continue running or catching balls they undoubtedly will but this does not mean that noticeable signs of weariness should be ignored.

The result of continually pushing your dog over his limit will be a restless, fidgety uncomfortable dog, who on reaching home, will pace, pick up toys and be unable to settle. This behaviour *does not* signal the need to increase exercise. If more exercise is implemented, it replaces the opportunity to sleep, and the body produces more adrenaline. Once the sympathetic nervous system is switched on it destroys the ability to sleep. This is why it is integral that a dog is allowed some down time when he is taken home. This facilitates relaxation and allows the parasympathetic system to take over and promotes homeostasis.

There are numerous other scenarios that can seriously affect a dogs' ability to sleep. It is important that beds are located in several areas of a house so a dog can choose where he wants to sleep. If the only bed available is in an area such as a busy kitchen, a dog will be continually disturbed.

Isolation can also have a big impact, and while crates may seem like a good thing they can cause distress and discomfort, particularly if a dog is unable to lie flat or he feels isolated from the family. Some people do successfully use crates, but they work hard at creating a very positive association. The door of a crate must always be left open and placed in an area of security and safety so a dog can rest there should he choose to. In the case of a multiple dog household, dogs may choose to sleep closely together, but they should not be expected to share one bed, because this can lead to severe disruption of sleep should one dog dislike sleeping in close proximately to the other.

Sleep can also be disrupted for other reasons, including being too cold or too hot, or the presence of pain or other serious diseases including diabetes, arthritis, anaemia, heart disease and canine cognitive dysfunction which can all be common as a dog ages.

Hunger and appetite can also be the cause of disrupted sleep. Research has shown that the two hormones that control appetite, leptin and ghrelin have a significant role in the story of sleep. Leptin signals a sense of feeling full while ghrelin triggers a strong sensation of hunger. When leptin is circulating in the blood, appetite is blunted, but when ghrelin levels increase so too does a desire to eat. Sleep deprivation directly affects these hormones, and ghrelin has been shown to be really active when sleep is inadequate, and without the right amount of sleep, the "full up" signal ceases to be switched on.

It is not a huge leap to understand why a dog that is not receiving sleep can seem to be "badly behaved", we know all too well that being continually hungry is not positive.

This is especially relevant in the case of recently rescued dogs that have not only found a kennel environment difficult, but upon being rehomed find themselves trying to adjust to with huge life changes and challenges. This is not a good time to be teaching a dog to sit and wait for his food. As stress levels drop, sleep becomes more normalised, and will contribute to balancing the hormones. This is the point at which learning can then take place.

<u>What can you provide to help your dog receive the right amount and quality of sleep?</u>

- Dogs need beds large enough for them to be able to lie flat, otherwise they cannot reach REM sleep. Hard sided donut shaped beds should be avoided as they force dogs to curl up into a ball, and this too prevents REM sleep.
- Dogs often like pillows, by providing one your dog can choose to use it or ignore it, but many dogs appreciate a pillow!
- Dogs are social sleepers, do not force your dog to sleep alone.
- They prefer warmth and elevation, which provide a sense of safety and comfort. If you are one of those people that allows your dog to sleep on your bed then give yourself a large pat on the back, this is of huge benefit to both of you!
- Do not force your dog to go hours without access to a toilet area.
- Hunger will affect sleep so feeding twice or even three smaller meals a day, instead of one large meal, will eliminate this problem (This is basic

information but some people do continue to feed their dogs only once a day)

Do not disturb your dog when he is sleeping. Let sleeping dogs lie!

Pancakes for dogs

Whilst we are making pancakes for ourselves you can also make a version for your dogs. I often make them for my dogs and use bananas and fruit as fillings but their most favourite is cooked black pudding

The recipe is as follows

50g plain flour

1 egg

100ml of water (or milk if your dog can tolerate it)

Mix the ingredients and whisk and then heat your pan with a little coconut oil, add the mixture and let it cook for around 30 seconds, then turn it and cook briefly on the other side.
Let the pancakes cool and then add bananas or blueberries or peanut butter (but make sure it is xylitol free) or some dogs even enjoy marmite or a similar product.
Obviously make sure you don't feed too many to your dog, or you may need to readjust the ingredients if your dog can't tolerate grain

Fear and reactivity.

Reactivity is a very common problem and many dogs are fearful and worried about meeting other dogs when out walking.

A dog can't be trained not to feel fear, although it is possible to punish a dog while he is fearful and cause him to shut down. If a dog does shut down this can appear to fix the situation and a dog may appear very compliant, but if this path is followed, it is likely to ruin a dogs' life, and result in a spiral of increasing fear and misery. It is said that dogs can react five times faster than we can (in actuality they are probably far faster than this) and the result can be that dogs have no option than to bark, leap, lunge, growl or even bite any dog in the vicinity that is perceived as a threat. The outcome of this is that an anxious dog may be saddled with the label of being aggressive, even though he is only trying to defend himself.

If this is a familiar scenario then time is your friend, and the winter is a good time of year to start finding a solution. Fear or extreme negative emotion is *not* easy to fix as it is often a slow burner. Our dogs are very good at telling us they are uncomfortable but in turn we are good at misreading situations.

The solution that many people advocate is to start a training programme but training is not a panacea and is unlikely to fix anything unless the root cause is addressed. There is a time and place for training but not if a dog is experiencing regular periods of extreme fear. The following points are often recommended as a solution but at best they are like plaster over an arterial wound

- Asking a dog to sit while dogs go past may stop him barking, for a while, but that dog *will* remain fearful.

- Offering treats might be of some use as a distraction but fear will remain. While there is no doubt this is a good coping strategy, it is at best overshadowing
- Using "look at me " training is unlikely to provide a solution as the fear and anxiety is not being addressed.

If we really want to help reactive dogs' we have to be more open minded. A dog needs to feel like he can rely on the person on the other end of the lead and needs a degree of choice, so he is able to distance himself by moving away. Communication is essential and this is why calming signals and/ or displacement activities help to defuse some of the worry and anxiety.

If a dog is extremely anxious about other dogs, the chance and opportunity to move away should always be available. Be prepared to stop exposing your dog to things he finds frightening, terrifying or frustrating and identify with your dog- how you would feel in a situation you find frightening?

Do you think being made to sit as a snake slithers past would help if you had an extreme fear of snakes? It is hugely unlikely because sitting as a snake moved by would make you vulnerable, and secondly you would be primed via your brain to lash out if that snake comes towards you, and possibly even attack the person who was insisting that you remain still.

Ultimately the fear area of your brain (the amygdala} starts to take over in place of rational thought.
Winter is a good time to work on building your dog's confidence, quite simply because there are less people and

dogs around.

Utilise the darker nights, arm yourself with hi-viz, attach lights to your clothing and search out well- lit areas such as car parks and make a start to restore your dog's confidence

Hygge for dogs?

It occurred to me the other day as I was reading a book about hygge (pronounced Hoo Ga) that the ideas behind it could be used for our dogs

The examples in the book sounded familiar in lots of ways

· Taking pleasure from the presence of soothing things

· The absence of annoyance

· Cosy togetherness

The author then went on to talk about hygge being with people you love, a feeling of home, a feeling that we are safe, that we are shielded from the world and can let our guard down. This feeling of shelter and safety is exactly what we should be striving to provide for our dogs.

Many people would dismiss this, but there are also many more people that feel this is exactly what they are trying to provide for their dogs, after all it can't just be a human thing to want to feel sheltered, safe and to be with friends we feel totally secure and comfortable with.

Hygge with your dogs!

Snow Angels

Sometimes in the UK we have a snowfall. It doesn't happen that often but when it does dogs react in many different ways. Most dogs welcome the pristine blanket of cold fluffy stuff but some dogs react very differently

There are some dogs that seem very dizzy and excited when they see a vastly changed environment and this may cause them to become uncertain and even overstimulated, but of course most dogs are full of glee. But if dogs are overwhelmed, it can look a lot like excitement and joy while the dogs themselves may feel confused and bewildered.

If your dog reacts to a changed snowy landscape by appearing a little frenzied and doesn't react quite how you anticipated it may not be happiness that he is experiencing. If you are unsure as to what is going on, the best course of action is to return to an area that has less snow cover and looks closer to "normal". If your dog seems relieved and becomes calm then this will give you a better interpretation as to what your dog may have been experiencing.

These reactions are more common than many of us would believe, and are likely to occur when dogs have less body awareness and are thrown by sensory challenges. It may be difficult to put the pieces of the puzzle together if your dog reacts to conditions in a way you weren't expecting, but if you witness your dog becoming frazzled then the best course of action is to move your dog away to a different area.

Snow in particular is not something that dogs see regularly in the UK, so we do need to be aware that they may not embrace it with as much enthusiasm as we may predict.

There is another surprising element that we may not be aware of in the winter when it is cold enough for snow or a heavy frost. Scent changes.

Dogs that are accustomed to inhaling scent in their everyday lives, especially those that are bred for their olfactory skills such as labradors or spaniels may find that their outside environment is a very different place to normal.

In the words of Kirsty Grant of the Dog Nose "hot smells" in a cold environment will stand out, so for example the scent of a human or rabbit that has left a fresh track will be easily detected but once a scent has reached an ambient temperature the effect will be lost. Dogs that come out into new snowfall might initially be excited because their normal busy olfactory world is less familiar and unbelievably "quiet"

It is always best to reserve judgement and not make assumptions about how your dog might react to vastly differing weather conditions

Hands off!

A dog's head belongs to the dog. This is why people should be discouraged from touching and stroking a dogs' head.

The dogs head has a vital role, it encases the brain and houses the following important systems and senses

- The brain
- Sight
- Hearing
- Smell
- 12 pairs of cranial nerves -including part of the vagus nerve and the trigeminal nerve.

These are crucial for your dog to be able to function and make "a dog" what he is. The head has a rich supply of important nerves including the trigeminal nerve which if damaged can become extremely painful and distressing.

The TMJ, or temporomandibular joint, which is located at the top of a dog's jaw has connections to important functions such as eating and balance, and if injured can become hypersensitive and cause extreme pain. This is why dogs are often protective of these areas and may duck away if someone stretches their hand out towards them. I do wish the general public would be more aware that dogs don't elect to be stroked on their heads, and the majority of dogs would instead choose to be touched on the sides of their body if at all.

There are many dogs that may greet people enthusiastically but may in fact dislike being touched so it is always best to advocate for your dog and ask people to stand quietly before they reach out to stroke your dog. Alternatively, you can take an even more positive approach and ask people *not* to touch your dog.

Allowing our dogs to decide and give their consent to being touched is beneficial for them, and they would certainly thank us for asking people to keep their hands off!

Some thoughts on winter from Laura Dobb of the Slow Dog Movement

This is about how soft humans have gotten and how this is making us, well, basically ill. I follow Wim Hof who talks about our immune systems and how many are rife with inflammation, and our lack of dopamine and he often talks

about the role of the autonomic nervous system.
Well, Wim Hof says he is not special, all of us can turn our health around.

Wim speaks about brain science, our immune system, stress and much more. It is so interesting. Wim Hof talks about his dog too! But it's true that we now lead lives which are radically different to how we should live. We are soft and our dogs live with us.

Dogs' fur coats are getting thinner because of their indoor life with central heating. We now have to put fleece coats on our dogs in the winter to help them regulate their temperatures when the weather is cold. Could it be that our dogs are also getting soft? After all, they are often stuck at home when we work, whether we are there or not. We take them on walks but panic if they get dirty.

I am not advocating that folks tie their dogs up outside and leave them there like the 'old days'. Not at all. But we share so much physiology with dogs and already have proof that their evolution has changed because of increased indoor life *and* they are suffering more and more from inflammatory diseases, due to environmental contaminants and food as well, just like us.

What am I suggesting? Well, it's made me think about my life with my dogs. I am usually a cold water swimmer. I am landlocked right now but am taking cold showers every day. We are living in a campervan in Yorkshire and are surrounded by trees. We were not surrounded by trees when we lived in Cornwall.

I had lost my sense of smell due to C19 but my sense of smell has come back since living near these glorious trees and amongst all the fallen leaves. A forest bathing benefit! I love the cold of Yorkshire. The snow and bitter winds we had on the weekend made me feel alive.

During my walks with my dogs during the weekend, I noticed that they were invigorated too. My terrier hates her coat, and I have realised she hates all coats. It may be a sensory integration thing. She just stops walking. She slows down so much that even I think it's too slow. But she has arthritis and shakes from it. I didn't put her coat on today and she was so full of vigour.

What shall we do for our dogs -and us? What can you think of that could improve our dogs' indoor existence?

Obviously allowing dogs to run through the puddles helps dogs to feel alive and in touch with their senses. I don't 'molly coddle' my dogs but I am going to start being even more conscious of their sensory world and experiences. If it snows again, I am going to make snow angels when my dogs are making snow dog angels!

Ageing canines

It is not lost on me that the seasons are synonymous with times in our lives and the winter is often related to senior years, so this next part is about ageing dogs

Ageing is not a disease and this is important to keep in mind as our dogs become older. What we feed them, how we exercise them, what beds we choose for them all have a huge impact on what kind of health they will enjoy as they become older. Just like humans, the early years have a direct and profound influence on the senior years. The later years are a reflection of every decision we make from the moment we pick the little wiggly puppy out from his litter mates.

As our dogs' lives reach into two figures we should take

an increased interest in how they are coping. We need to consider our dogs daily routines and be quick to alter anything that seems to have a detrimental effect. Certainly our expectations of our dogs need to be taken into account before we cause them distress.

We should not necessarily make changes to diet or cut down on favourite foods as they turn nine, as is often advocated, but it is a good idea to take short video clips every month in order to track any changes in movement. Not only should movement patterns be monitored but carers with older dogs should get into the habit of checking their dogs carefully and mindfully by running their hands over all the body to check for increased heat or to look for any "giveaways" including odd reactions to touch in specific areas. Search for patches of ruffled hair (which can denote muscle spasms), changes in how they toilet- including not being able to squat while pooping, or only lifting one specific leg to urinate (if you have a dog) or a preference for different foods (to normal) or less enthusiasm when out walking. These points cover dogs of all ages but start to become really important as our dogs age, as their health and/ or immune systems may become less robust.

The odd thing is that it is very possible for different areas of the body to age at different rates. For example, it can often be difficult to estimate how old a dog is just by looking at their faces, as a black dog may start to go grey around the muzzle as early as 4 years old. Generally, it is true that older dogs become less active, but this is compounded if pain issues are present.

We should keep track of behaviour as this can signal discomfort, for instance this might manifest itself by a dislike of being touched, as this is a red flag particularly if a dog has previously craved being petted and fussed. Other areas to note are variations in sleep patterns, or loss of appetite. This can occur naturally as the sense of taste and smell becomes less acute with age, but it is of importance if it occurs suddenly.

There may also be changes within the body's homeostatic mechanisms. If the body is less able to regulate temperature, then a dog may experience difficulty with a "normal" everyday life especially as the seasons shift. This is also why older dogs are more likely to suffer from dehydration in the summer. While this list is often presented if a dog is in pain, it cannot be stressed strongly enough that these become far more serious as dogs age. Owners are often blind to these things and will carry on doing the same walks and exercise as they have always done long after they should have been altered.

Loss of muscle is also often overlooked. This often occurs in the hind legs which are important for locomotion. A dog already carries around 60% of his weight on the front legs so any increase will become a burden very rapidly. Older dogs are less able to re-build muscle, and if they compensate and shift weight to the front legs then muscle will quickly atrophy. Less muscle means loss of muscle tone. An older dog with muscle atrophy will tire rapidly during walks, this is why exercise is a lynchpin when caring for older dogs. This does not mean walks need to cease but they just need to be tailored to ensure they don't cause distress. Taking an older dog out remains important for mental and physical health, and shorter walks do not have to be boring.

The following things can be weaved into walks; for

instance, short distances through slightly longer grass, or find sandy areas which provide grip and are good for cushioning joints, as long as the sand isn't too deep and the perfect time will be at the beach at low tide. Slight inclines, or using wide gentle low steps can help to maintain fitness without over taxing a dog that is beginning to struggle with "normal" walks, but remain vigilant as fatigue is not an easy thing for an older dog to deal with. This also prevents the hearts and lungs being overtaxed as these too can deteriorate as dogs age. Appropriate exercise also contributes to burning calories but this does become more sluggish with age. It is very likely that arthritis has occurred somewhere in the body, which is why vet checks should become an integral part of an older dog's life.

Overweight older dogs are also likely to suffer from issues due to overloading of the joints, but this is the same for any age of dog. Do tailor nutrition as the wrong foods not only cause obesity but can have devastating effects on a dogs' wellbeing. Some people believe that protein levels should be reduced as dogs age, but do remember why protein is needed. Unless a dog has a specific health problem, protein is as important for an older dog as it is for a younger dog.

Protein is both incredibly complex and integral to continued good health, it assists with the building and repairing of muscle, is needed to form more skin cells and grow hair and has a role with creating hormones and enzymes which are needed for essential functions. Without adequate protein the body will deteriorate. Reducing levels without consulting your vet is not a sensible decision to make, and can cause spiralling health issues.

Older dogs are also more likely to suffer from hormonal changes due to degeneration. This does not in itself make older dogs ill, but this is another reason for careful monitoring. The smell of their breath also changes with age, due to gastrointestinal slowdown, this may not solely be as a result of tooth decay, but can also be a symptom of the gut working less efficiently. This may also be accompanied by decreased production of saliva which is needed to clean the mouth; this in turn can have a harmful effect on the teeth. Many older dogs do have a build- up of plaque on the teeth, but if they have had suitable oral management and lots of good healthy chews throughout their lives, this can be avoided and is less likely to be a problem. Oral decay is not a given, unless it wasn't prioritised earlier in life.

Health issues can also include incontinence, due to malfunction of the bladder. This is often noticeable if wet patches appear on beds or random puddles on the floor are seen. It is at this stage when many people believe their dogs have forgotten their house training, but this is rare. It is more commonly due to arthritic changes in the spine or the result of the sphincter muscles that control urination becoming weaker. Medications are available and can be useful if this occurs and a vet can advise you on options. Some of the drugs now available are very successful in helping with urinary incontinence. Never underestimate how difficult it is for our dogs to have to deal with incontinence, try not to make a fuss as this can be really distressing for the dog, and contribute to their anxiety. Incontinence will accompany Canine Cognitive Disease (CCD), and it is true that many dogs may not understand what is happening if they succumb to this disease, but it does not make it any less comfortable to live with. Urine burns dogs just as surely as it does humans, and double incontinence adds another potential for worry and stress.

Sleep is another area which needs vigilance. Even if an older dog is not suffering from CCD sleep patterns can alter significantly. Older dogs tend to sleep much deeper and for increased periods of time, and there are moments when it can be difficult to see the ribcage rising and falling. Good beds are indispensable, and slightly elevated beds are indicated (if the dog finds it easy to climb on and off) as beds on the floor can be cold and draughty. Getting in and out quickly and easily will also be a priority as a dog ages, so be aware that really soft beds might become traps. If an older dog shows a reluctance to use a bed he has formerly loved, then this might be the time to select an orthopaedic bed which provides joint support and comfort while being firm enough to provide support.

When all is said and done what makes the biggest impact on an older dog's life is us. We need to make time for our older dogs. The value of sitting with them, providing care and love, especially when health is impaired, cannot be underestimated. All they want is for us to be with them, and to do anything less is to desert them when we are most needed. One of the nicest ways of doing this is to take an outing to a favourite place. Take a drink and a picnic for both of you, and enjoy being in a quiet peaceful place where you can both just "be".

Every day is precious and even if there are no known health problems it is not something you will ever regret doing.

Christmas. A sensory onslaught

This is the time of year that we need to advocate for our dogs, there is a lot going on which is not part of normal life plus the hype around Christmas can be considerable. As far as dogs are concerned there is an increase in sensory stimuli during this period which can prove intolerable.

Let's have a think about what we subject our dogs to

Auditory
Music and more noise from electronics such as tablets and TV's and loud excited voices. While carols may be soothing, turning the volume up on old pop favourites is not!

Olfactory
Christmas trees, especially if they are "real"
Cooking and delicious smelling novel foods
Fragranced candles, please do remember that dogs can't tolerate perfumed candles. If they are used, please make sure your dog has another area he can escape to. It is not only candles either as there are many other situations where a dog will encounter strong aromas including from visitors that delight in wearing their favourite, often overpowering perfumes and aftershaves or may carry disturbing scents on their clothes or within their own bodies.

We are likely to be unaware of potential problems with our comparatively poor sense of smell.

Visual

Flashing lights and decorations the presence of a tree with presents under it and tempting things hanging off it
Flashing lights both in the home and outside when walking
Some dogs, especially young puppies, or rescues, or even older dogs may find it very uncomfortable when furniture is moved around to accommodate extra people and decorations.
Cleaning and general rushing about also add to visual overload and can contribute to overstimulation

Gustatory

Unusual rich foods. Please make sure that any visitors are aware of what could cause GI upsets if given to dogs, and visitors should be made aware of how dangerous specific foods such as chocolate and some nuts can be to dogs.

Plus

- There is a potential that there is just too much going on which is outside of a dogs' comprehension.
  Don't let people interact with your dog and tell him what to do. It is unfair. For some reason there always seems to be one visitor that has strong opinions on how dogs should behave and takes the role on of "dog whisperer".
- The amount of food present in homes will create frustration particularly as the constant cooking and lovely smells are tempting and overwhelming to any dog. Make sure your dog gets fed at normal

times and that he has a little taste of the delicious food (unless of course it is unsuitable or toxic)
- Advocate for your dog. He is part of the family too. Provide an area in advance where he knows he can relax and will not be disturbed.
  Visitors should understand this too, especially any visiting children. However much a dog likes them he must be protected, and in turn children should not be allowed to seek dogs out and pester them. This is an essential conversation that should be discussed with any visitors no matter if they are only present for an hour or the entire festive period.
  Once a dog has removed himself from a room, he should be free to return only when he is ready.

Not all dogs want to be the life and soul of the party and can find it really hard to cope. This is the main reason why so many dogs are surrendered to rescues and shelters after Christmas is over, often through no fault of their own.

More tips for the holiday season

As previously discussed, Christmas can be exceedingly difficult for dogs.

Here are a few more pre-Christmas thoughts and pointers for helping your dog cope with the festive season.

Remember it's your dog's home as much as it is yours

Visitors are not always as accommodating as you might be, so please don't allow guests to tell you how your dog should behave, or insist on sitting on your dog's favourite place on the sofa. It's not fair if your dog is suddenly demoted by guests and visitors.

Make sure your dog has a place of sanctuary

Don't expect your dog to 'be social' and stay in the same room with guests. If he is uncomfortable or needs a bit of space then he must be able to seek out a quiet place where he can go and remain undisturbed.

If children are present in the house, please put a visible boundary a few feet away from your dog's main resting area (such as a very visible strip of duct tape) and tell them they must not step over this boundary to reach the dog.

Keep to a normal diet

Things can be added into a dog's normal food like bits of turkey, freshly cooked vegetables and maybe some roast potatoes but don't overdo it. Rich food is no better for our dogs than it is for us.

Treats and presents should be vetted

If people buy presents for your dog, please check them! Highly coloured rawhide shaped into candy canes and boots, or novelty foods such as 'doggy mince pies', can be toxic or dangerous.

There are still many products available for dogs which originate from places like China and which are sold in pound shops. They are often made from rawhide and are soaked in chemicals and pose a health risk if ingested. The best place for these gifts is your bin, not in your dog, please dispose of them at the first possible opportunity.

Walks should be for your dog
Boxing Day walks are very popular with many families. Crowds can be really stressful for your dog, on top of all the other disruptions, particularly if your daily routine walks are low key or if your dog doesn't socialise much with other dogs or people.

Make sure you maintain normal daily walks, and allow your dog to sniff, explore and just spend some time with you. If you are accompanied on your walks don't let children hijack your dog or make them run or play games. Neither should 'show and tell' type obedience tricks be part of your dog's schedule to entertain guests. Children should be taught to allow dogs to choose whether they want to interact with them and understand they are not playthings.

Don't leave your dog alone for hours while you are visiting friends or family
The other side of the coin can be just as distressing. Dogs should not be left for extended periods of time because you have social functions to attend. If you have a long

away day planned do make arrangements with neighbours or friends for your dog to be let out to stretch his legs and take regular toilet breaks.

Isolation is just as bad for our dogs as having to cope with a house stuffed full of people.

Are you visiting relatives or friends with your dog?
Make sure your dog is not exposed to people that only just tolerate him and have expectations that can't possibly be upheld.

It is at these times that it is a good idea to stay somewhere nearby like a holiday cottage so that you all have some downtime away from too many expectations.

A Dog For All Seasons

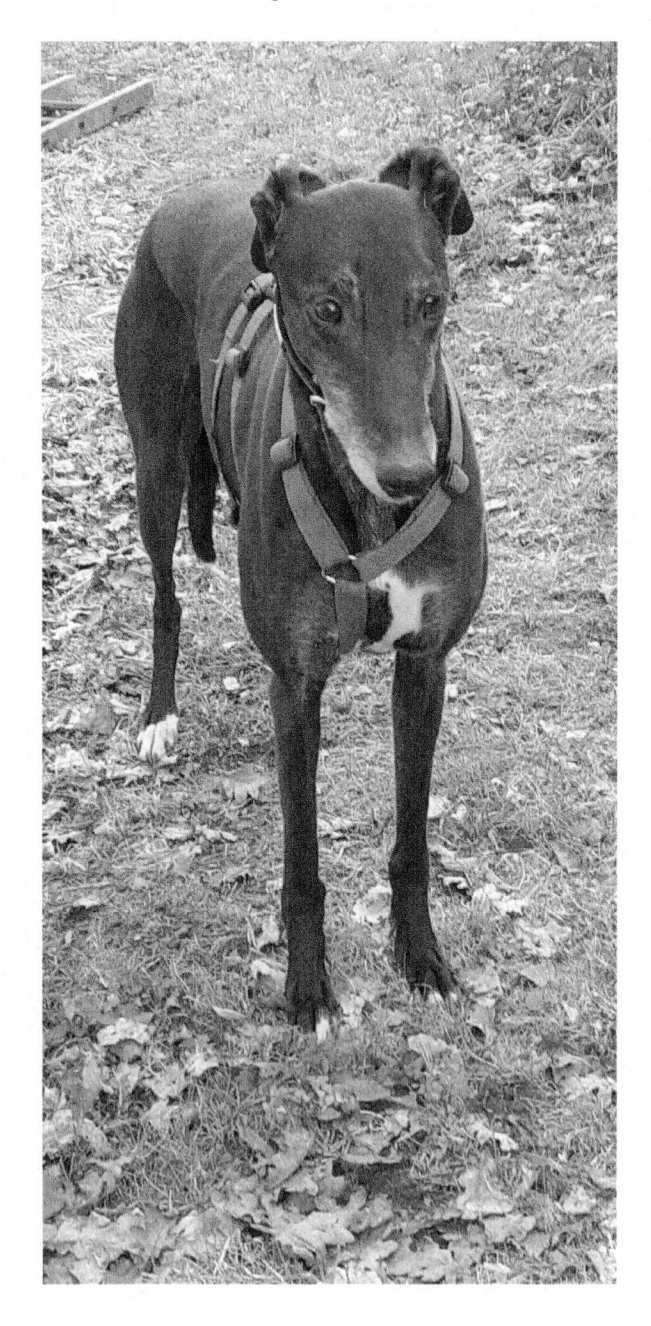

ANYTIME OF THE YEAR

This chapter has been included because the topics are important and equally pertinent no matter what time of year. Although the book is sprinkled with anecdotes and other thoughts which are not necessarily relevant to the season they were inserted in, on reflection it seemed to be a good idea to have a separate chapter which includes other facets of our lives with dogs.

FOREST BATHING WITH YOUR DOG.

Imagine it is a lovely warm sunny day and you are out with your dog. You step into a leafy wood and walk along narrow paths that are dappled with sunshine. The trees are tall and wide and you feel you are almost completely submerged in soft green light. Your dog sniffs and you feel no need to hurry, as the environment encourages you to slow down, pause, and to take deep breaths as you look up to where the trees stop and where you can see patches of blue sky through the canopy.

Welcome to Forest Bathing with your dog.

Let's go back a few steps. Many people are conditioned about how to walk their dogs. They follow the unwritten rules and ideas that are advocated which include two walks a day which comprise of running, socialising with other dogs and perhaps a bit of sniffing thrown in.

A Dog For All Seasons

Many people feel they are doing the right thing for their dogs, but it has been proven via the canine ethogram that this formulaic way of exercising dogs is not actually what many dogs would choose. Dogs are very social but their basic needs extend beyond daily exercise, feeding and general overseeing. It can be difficult to get people to become more aware that there are inadequacies in what they provide for their dogs in their daily lives. Many of us are so preoccupied with our everyday routines that there is little time to think about whether we could further improve the lives of our dogs.

This is not to say that the needs of dogs are ignored but rather how with a bit of thought we could enhance not only our dogs' lives but our own health and wellbeing.

To explain in more detail, we need to return to the canine ethogram. This has been studied at length but the details have not become general knowledge for many dog owners. It contains a lot of information about how dogs would live their lives if they were able to choose. Research has been undertaken in areas of the world where dogs are free roaming and has found that their days are spent very differently to how we might predict. They very rarely run, spend only a little time in play, they mingle with people but spend the majority of their lives in loose groups that are fluid and non- confrontational. They rarely fight and when they do it is not often about the things that we might envisage. In fact, their lives are fairly peaceful, and more importantly stress is not commonly reported.

If this is true of semi feral dogs lives how can we replicate elements of this more balanced way of life for our own dogs?

The idea of Forest Bathing is relatively new, and it was

the Japanese, who are so often way ahead of European culture that discovered how important it was to spend time interacting with nature.

This might surprise many of us that think of Japan as being a place with large cities where millions of people live, but In 1982 the science of Forest Bathing (or Shinrin - Yoku) began in the Akasawa Forest in Japan. This was in part a campaign to save the forests, but it also had another important effect, that of promoting healing and to increase the wellbeing of the population through nature.

In 2004 this began to come to the attention of the rest of the world, and scientific research started to make the link between human health and forests. As a direct consequence of these studies 62 certified Forest Therapy bases were established in Japan, and now in the present day there are 31 Forest Bathing Guides in the UK, and 11 in Southern Ireland.

It is not a huge leap to include our dogs when we think about the benefits of Forest bathing and there is now a book called "Forest Bathing with your Dog" which outlines how a connection to nature could be shared alongside our dogs.

Having established why it is of immense value, how do we start practising it? Forget the images that might flit through your mind of thousands of acres of forest in faraway places, and hours of hiking before you can reach the right place. If you went out with a guide you would experience something very different. A guided walk might last 2 – 4 hours but may often cover no more than a quarter of a mile. But we don't necessarily need a guide because suitable areas are very likely to be within easy reach of our homes. Instead of spending hours travelling to the right locations in our cars, spaces can be found nearby which allow us to use our senses and encourage our dogs to drop their heads and immerse themselves in the sounds and smells of nature.

Neither do we need lots of fancy equipment, travel light and dress according to the weather. If it is cold wear thin layers of clothes, or grab a hat if it is hot, take water for you and your dog and a snack for yourself and a chew for your dog. Take a light blanket for both of you to sit on; turn your phone off and put it in a back pack, this is because interruptions are unwelcome. A harness and a long line are recommended for dogs as this helps to keep commands to a minimum, and help to allow the full force of nature to work its magic. Instead of dictating the direction to your dog just let him choose but slow yourself down. These all contribute and enhance the quality of the experience and help us to immerse ourselves in nature. The slower you move, the lower the heart rate becomes and this in turn allows breathing to become slower and deeper for both yourself and your dog.

Walk without an agenda or a plan, and start to examine what is around you. In this environment dogs will automatically start to sniff more deeply and this allows you to take cues from your dog. As you walk you will find natural "sit" spots. These are places where you are able to break from walking and offer your dog his chew while you relax and take in the rhythm of the woods which surround you.

Nature has a way of inviting you in, for instance not many people are aware that the tree canopy if full of fractals. These are complex patterns which occur everywhere in nature and are scientifically proven to induce relaxation, research shows that exposure to fractal patterns in nature reduce stress in humans by up to 60%. It is thought that stress reduction occurs because of a certain physiological resonance within the eye. It is not just tree canopy's which are rich in them, they are also found in snowflakes, shells and flower petals. All this becomes more profound if you are accompanied with your dog.

The overall benefits are enormous and for humans they include

- An increase in energy
- Decrease in anxiety, depression and anger
- Lowering of stress
- Improvement in concentration and memory
- Improves pain thresholds
- Helps with loss of weight
- Can improve sleep

This is not where the story stops, it continues with the benefits for our dogs which include-

- Woodland forest floor is low impact which makes it good for older dogs with limited abilities
- Can reduce fear in dogs that are nervous around people (especially newly rescued dogs) and gives them much needed space
- Positive ions from inhaling fresh air (household chemicals can have an adverse effect on our dogs)
- Grounding via the earth's low impulse of electromagnetic energy
- Relaxation and stress relief from inhaling deeply and sniffing.

- Low impact exercise from climbing onto fallen logs, rocks and stumps and walking through rivers and streams.
- Sunlight provides Vit D
- Boosts confidence through movement and additionally these activities increase the bond between us and our dogs.

As we explore and immerse ourselves in nature our dogs mirror our own emotional states. This can create big changes and benefits even if you are only able to spend a few hours a week in woodland or forest. The elements of forest bathing can be bought into most any walk but the biggest benefit comes from regular longer sessions. It is also possible to nature bathe by the sea just as long as you use your senses and you allow your dog to do the same.

As the world becomes progressively busier Forest Bathing helps us to slow down, commune with nature and teaches us to spend more quality time with our dogs

LET YOUR DOG SNIFF!

It is hard to imagine what it would be like to be a dog. What we do know is that they perceive the world around them very differently to us.

Our main method of gathering information is to use our eyes to monitor what is around us. When we wake up every morning, sight is our primary sense, and then only when we have taken stock with our eyes might we use our nose, primarily if someone is cooking breakfast, or making coffee but this is always secondary to "checking in" with our eyes. Not so with dogs, their sense of smell very rarely switches off-to live in the world of the dog is a world filled with scent.

This is important to understand on many levels. We are all aware of some of the astounding facts. For example, a dogs' nose is so sensitive that it is possible for a trained dog to detect a human body in a depth of over 80 foot of water. A dogs' sense of smell is 10,000 to 100, 000 times better than ours. James Walker, former director of Florida State University Sensory Research Institute, has a useful way of explaining how well developed a dogs' sense of smell is "If you make an analogy to vision, what you and I can see at a third of a mile, a dog could see more than 3,000 miles away and still see well". These amazing feats are possible because dogs have very specialised nasal anatomy.

Most of this is not visible, but what can be seen is a nose which is typically wet or moist. This is important as this helps capture moisture and dissolve molecules which are in the air around the dog. The two nostrils, or nares, are able to function independently of each other, and sniffing is accomplished by a series of short inhalations and exhalations. When a dog takes a sharp inward breath the nostrils change shape, allowing air into the upper area of the nose. During this phase air can be siphoned out, or kept in the dogs' nose with a very specialised bit of equipment. The dogs' nose has a special flap which can be closed if he wants to retain a scent, while any scents that he doesn't want can be expelled as normal through the side of either nostril.

The odour is then passed to an area of bony, ruffle like structures called the turbinates. These little scroll- like structures sift out molecules and pass them onto the olfactory area of the dogs' brain. This area can also serve as a filter to trap bacteria via the mucous that lines them.

It is the posterior area of the turbinate bones that contains the 300 million olfactory receptors, needed to recognise odour molecules. These receptors have tiny hair like structures called cilia which relay signals to the area of the brain that is dedicated to olfaction, the olfactory bulb.

The olfactory bulb is really well developed. This area of the dogs' brain is far larger than a humans. While our brains are dominated by a huge visual cortex, a dogs' brain has evolved a large area to sift through the important information generated by scent.

What is interesting is that this area of the brain has a direct link to the limbic system. Why is this important for us dog owners to understand? Because this area of the brain is very primitive and deals with emotions, memory and behaviour.

As humans, we are able understand this a little if a particularly evocative smell sends us to a particular place and time, and prompts vivid memories. If this is how *we* experience specific smells, then we may have a very small window into how this can influence a dogs' mind and stimulate instinctive reactions to his world. Because we now have a better understanding of how a dogs' nose functions- we can also appreciate how a dogs' sense of smell shapes his world.

Scent also travels to other more recent/ modern areas of the brain which have a role in conscious thought, and which may also contribute to a dogs' actions and behaviour. This, to a dog, is very powerful.

But this is not where the story ends. There is an additional area above the roof of a dogs' mouth which is called the Jacobsons organ, or vomeronasal organ, this detects body scents and pheromones. Dogs are able to pick up these odours by sniffing other dogs "smelly" areas. These are the actions that we, as humans, are very uncomfortable with. Genital areas, mouths, and anal areas, are a veritable mine of information regarding breeding status, health, and how the body, of the dog they are examining is functioning.

This becomes even more uncomfortable if we are getting the once over by a dog pressing his nose into our groins. We have become inhibited about these things as our "social skills" have increased. But, for a dog these areas contain a rich source of detailed information, and unless a dog dislikes being examined around these areas, we should always allow our dogs to perform this ritual like behaviour.

This is a very brief and simple summary of how well developed a dogs' sense of smell is, but why is it so integral to physical and mental wellbeing?

A dog needs to smell in order to gather information about what, and who is around him. He can also find out why things happened and how, just from one simple deep inhalation. To deny a dog the luxury of dropping his nose, taking deep breaths and observing the world in this way, is akin to us being blindfolded when taken out to see a view or go sightseeing.

When your dog steps out of your house to begin a walk his nose is already in overdrive, he is able to pick up on things we could never dream of. The change of seasons must be overwhelming to a dog, from the hot dusty lazy breezes of summer which must bring scents to noses in an almost meandering fashion, to the heady smells of autumn filled with leaves and musty decaying vegetation-these must be amazingly heady.

This is why the use of equipment or training techniques that prevent your dog sniffing are detrimental. Not only does your dog need to examine, perhaps minutely, the pile of leaves at his feet but his posture signals a sense of calm to any other dogs in the vicinity.

Sniffing is also a method of communication.

Think of a highly excited dog, pumped up with adrenaline. This picture is opposite to a dog with his head down, and the relaxed slightly raised tail of the sniffing canine. This body language is easy to identify for any dog in the area, as well as us "slow" humans! It denotes a sense of calm and of a dog just "doing his thing" This is particularly important for dogs that are worried and feel threatened by other dogs when out walking.

Reactive dogs (as they are often labelled) should always be allowed to sniff, and this activity should be actively encouraged by owners. Earlier in this article we touched on the limbic system. If the brain becomes increasingly alarmed, the results can become extreme. The body readies itself for fight or flight, and in some cases these extreme reactions are difficult to switch off. This is easy to see in fearful dogs, and areas of the brain can become highly attentive to certain situations. This is why our bodies (dogs and human) function so well when we perceive danger. But this is not how we would choose to lead our lives.

Not only is sniffing a great coping strategy but it also helps to reverse the effect that fear has on the brain. Sniffing has the ability to calm the emotions and help your dog to to stay relaxed while he is moving around in a dog rich environment, however unpredictable that may be.

Sniffing has links to wellbeing, and is a natural activity. This is why training methods should always be positive and include allowing dogs to investigate and explore the areas they are walking in. A dogs' head belongs to the dog, not to the human on the end of the lead; and it should never be rudely pulled up because they are "not paying attention" to us.

Training a dog should promote and use natural dog behaviours, not work against them. More people are becoming aware of the fact that using techniques to train their dogs that are against the dogs' nature cause anguish.

Yes, a dog will comply if people are advised to use harsh training techniques, but the anxiety this causes is not in the interest of the dog. A mechanised reaction to an owner's request is not obedience, it is subservience. Is that what we really require of our dogs?

It is time for us to look more closely at the innate behaviours of our dogs and to encourage them, rather than try to make their actions fit into our model of how we think our dogs should behave.

In short, taking your dog out on sniffing adventures and sniffy walks enhances the bond between you and your dog, and helps our dogs live their "best lives".

WHAT IS A DOG?

"Fall in love with a dog, and in many ways you enter a new orbit, a universe that features not just new colours but new rituals, new rules, a new way of experiencing attachment."
– Caroline Knapp

A Dog For All Seasons

When I posed the question "What is a Dog" in a Facebook group I run there were the many and varied replies to the question "what is a dog". These included the phrases "unconditional love", "opportunistic scavengers", "faithful", "reliant on us", and "man's best friend". Without doubt these are interesting but they reflect more on what we feel about dogs rather than actually addressing the question.

If we turn our attention to what we see there would be different answers. For instance, they might include observations on coat colour, movement, or behaviour.

Dogs are a sum of many parts and any one of the systems could be used in order to arrive at an answer. A dog has circulatory, skeletal and muscular systems as well as an ability to emote and experience the world. They also have basic inelastic needs including water, food and company, as well as more complex needs which we as care givers should understand and cater for.

Dogs are animals that have elected to live with us in our world. This is different from other species like horses or oxen that were initially employed by humans for specific jobs such as transport or food. So, their adoption of our world is surprising and a bit of a mystery. Maybe as one of my contributors suggested it is because they really are opportunistic scavengers?

Even if this is definitive, which it is not, we often forget just how specialised dogs are. Many people that have dogs are not particularly interested or aware of just how amazing they are, which is sad. They are so much "more" than a waggy tail with liquid eyes.

We need to go back to the very beginning of our collaboration to look into just how specialised they are, but this is tricky as nobody really knows when that was. Guesses vary from between 14,000 to 29,000 years ago. Either way they have been with us for a considerable chunk of time. This is why it is of concern that people do not understand dogs on a basic level.

Let's start with some facts that are widely known including the following- the scientific name for dogs- Canis familiairis, their diet- omnivore, their height- varies from 6-33 inches at the shoulder, and weight- 2 to 79 kilos. Although these are general facts, we can say that there is no such thing as a "standard" dog. They have become so varied and diverse that it would be hard to describe a dog to someone that had never seen one before.

Dogs do seem to love our company but that does not mean they love unconditionally, and neither should we expect loyalty. This is one of those "Disney myths" that people love to trot out in casual conversations. This idea of love is though- a factor that attracts people to bring dogs into their lives.

The oxytocin that is released when we look into the eyes of our own dogs is pretty powerful. However, this is not our due when we give a dog a home.

Following on from this line of thought it has been long debated about whether dogs have souls. Humans have certainly come a long way since the time of Descartes, and his beliefs. For those of us that have lived with dogs, this is probably a given, and every one of us will have stories that seem to indicate that dogs possess a soul. While this is unlikely to ever be proved one way or another, most people will testify to seeing their dogs grieve when a friend, whether dog or human passes. If this constitutes the presence of a soul then we already have an answer to this question, but their internal feelings and thoughts are very much theirs and only theirs and this status is likely to remain so for a very long time.

Even now we still don't have a firm grasp on what a dog is. A quadruped can be any size or shape and all have a similar kind of "blueprint". All mammals need systems in order to live in the world. However, dogs are one of the few animals that are bred to our specifications. There are different shapes and sizes of most animals, but none so varied as dogs. This has occurred without affecting their ultimate "dogness". The odd thing is that although they have become so diverse not every breed of dog is easily recognisable to other dogs.

For instance, greyhounds that race have only ever been surrounded by other greyhounds. It is not uncommon to have to introduce them to the idea that some of the smaller breeds are actually dogs. It can take months, or even years after rehoming before they correctly identify these breeds as members of their own species.

Despite these exceptions, (which are our fault and certainly not the fault of our dogs), we have a very specialised creature that can adapt to live in our world and happily absorb our lifestyles providing we don't mess things up. This is the point where we need to pause.

Dogs come complete with inherited genes, many of which have "highlighted" and enhanced via human modification to display traits which we value. By meddling we have without doubt made their lives more difficult. Many of the things we have selected and bred for have caused distress and have proved to be detrimental.

Is it so surprising then that dogs do things which we dislike? It is easy to blame them for behaviours which are out of *their* control. Specific health problems have been created via breeding for specific features which make their lives incredibly difficult . The shape of a dogs head should never have been interfered with, and neither should puppies ever be bred from mothers that are ill, stressed or psychologically damaged. These dogs will never fulfil their "dogness potential".

While looking at this from a pessimistic angle, there is no doubt that despite our Frankenstein interventions dogs still surprisingly continue to be dogs. They have an ability to adapt to new situations and our foibles with ease. Neophilia is not something that many species exhibit, and it is just as well that dogs come equipped with this ability.

Just to prove they are ultimate survivors google the story of the stray dogs in Moscow that have learnt how to navigate the underground systems and have become very adept at living in this very specific environment.
It's probably not all that surprising as dogs can become truffle hunters, are able to flush birds, herd sheep or become sheep guarders.

This is not bad for an opportunistic scavenger! We in turn have to acknowledge their natural behaviours instead of trying to supress them and change them into a subservient being. But with this history behind them it is unlikely that dogs will ever become another chapter in the story of human stupidity. We may not be able to come to a definitive answer but dogs are ultimate survivors!

https://abcnews.go.com/International/Technology/stray-dogs-master-complex-moscow-subway-system/story?id=10145833

APPENDIX

Just for a bit of fun these activities have been included which both you and your dog might find fun throughout the year

No 1

Take a good look at your dog, but don't be too intense as dogs often don't like being stared at

Look and observe your dog to see what is "normal"

Here are some pointers to help you

Take a look at how your dog naturally stands

This includes thinking about whether your dog finds it easy to keep his weight balanced equally on all four feet (not all dogs do find this easy). You may already know your dog has arthritis or mobility problems, but that doesn't stop you looking at how he stands or moves.

Look for muscle wastage or atrophy or collapsed wrists or unevenness in the body including less muscle on one side and overall posture.

Look at all four feet does one or more turn out?

Taking pictures and video is really useful, although you might want to ask someone else to take it as you walk your dog (as it is not easy on your own)

Take a look and check how your dog is moving- does he walk, pace or do a mixture of both?

Re-assess your dog at intervals as this will give you valuable information as the months and years tick past.

No. 2

Find somewhere you have never walked your dog before, it doesn't have to be exciting or have an amazing view. Do a bit of research and perhaps look at a local map as you may have overlooked some places of interest, or alternatively let your dog lead a walk and see where that takes you both. I have found lots of new places just by allowing my dogs to show me

   Most dogs don't care where they walk becaue it is all about their amazing senses.

They get far more from a walk by selecting their own areas. *We* might find the areas boring but this is not about us-it is about our dogs

Any new area can be very local or might involve a car journey.

No. 3

Find a bank or a fence and think about how you could ask your dog to do something that is a little unusual

Walk alongside a bank-rather than up and down

Or

Underneath a fence (for those of you with greyhounds it can take them a while to think about-as often this is not something that occurs to them)

or

walk along a wall

this will be easier for the smaller dogs than the ones that have long skinny legs.

Be aware that these activities should not be repeated

continually but seen as new activities and skills.

No. 4

Platters for your dog

Find some nice tasty different foods you think your dog might like and let him chose his favourites.

Use a muffin tin or a large plate where the foods can be spread out so they don't touch so that your dog can select and savour them individually.

You could include berries, cheese, different types of meat, boiled egg, sausages whatever you think your dog might enjoy, only small amounts are needed

As "dessert" you can also let your dog have a choice of chews, for instance tripe sticks, pizzles, fish skins or whatever you can source.

No. 5

As you are walking have a careful look to see if you can find anything that can be picked up and taken home with you for your dog to investigate at a later time or on another day

For example, feathers, or gloves that people have dropped, or old toys that people sometimes leave outside their doors that are no longer played with by the children of the house. Or take a clean cloth with you and rub it over a tree trunk, or gather some soil, or a few sticks and leaves for your dog to have a sniff at later

Take some bags as you walk as you can keep all the bits separate otherwise the scent will mix together and gradually fade and make them less interesting

No. 6

Does your dog have a favourite brush? Dogs don't always like being brushed, depending on whether they have had any negative experiences

This task is about finding a brush your dog likes, but **not** a functional one that removes mud/ thistles or mats etc

Not everything we do with our dogs has to be "functional" we also need to provide things that our dogs just enjoy. You might already know that your dog dislikes being brushed in which case just use your hands

The benefits of using your hands is that you are better able to identify any odd lumps or hotspots that might be present in your dog's body.
Use long slow strokes over the areas where your dog is most comfortable and enjoys the sensation, but don't work over areas that you know your dog doesn't like.

This is to provide your dog with a pleasureable experience the tactile sense is very important to our dogs

If you use your hands, check the fascia (layers of your dog's skin) for lumps and bumps and hotspots.

Check if your dog is correctly hydrated by gently picking up a little bit of skin between your first finger and thumb and gently lift it, it should spring back immediately, if not and it forms a little tent and takes a while to disappear your dog is dehydrated.

No.7

This is an observation task.

Some dogs walk and move so lightly over the floor you

can barely hear or see what they do. This is because they have good proprioception and spatial awareness.

But not all dogs have this.

Many like us are quite frankly a bit clumsy and are never really thoughtful about where they put their feet, so observe how lightly your dog moves.

Is your dog clumsy or does he seem to put a lot of thought into where he steps and how he moves?

It's not the most complex task but you will have to really watch your dog moving, you might also become more aware of how important tails are in aiding a dogs' balance or you may detect that your dog turns easier to the left than the right (or vice versa)

This might also change if your dog is inside or outside

If you feel your dog impacts on the ground quite heavily you might set up an area of softer footing but *NOT* too deep. The idea is for him to think carefully about how he negotiates it (an example might include an area with a duvet on it, or something else that has a sponge like texture)

RESOURCES

This is a brief round up of resources and references which may be of interest and have been mentioned at points throughout the book

Enrichment centres

Throughout the book I have mentioned enrichment centres these are a few that have been set up by canine professionals.

Crabtree Canine Enrichment (Sensory Adventure for Dogs), Crowborough, East Sussex

Pennie Clayton

Website-www.horseandhoundschool.co.uk

Snuffl, Scarborough 64, Eastbourough Scarborough

Laura Dobb

Website-snuffl.dog

Kirsty Grant

The Dog Nose Swindon Uk

REFERENCES

Spring

Sensory Integration for Dogs-check out www.freedogz.be

The study on street dogs which was mentioned -Majamber et al 2016

Amber Batson take a look at her Facebook page titled "Understand Animals".

Summer

In "Extinct" I discuss what might happen to dogs if humans were removed from the planet. I had written this section before the publication of a book by Marc Beckoff and Jessica Pierce. Find the details of in the book section

Autumn

The Bowen Technique

ww.thebowentechnique.com

Winter

Worm counts-www.wormcount.com

Hypermobility in dogs study
Title-First evidence for an association between joint hypermobility and excitability in a non human species, the domestic dog

Authors-Jonathon Bowen et al 2019

https://www.nature.com/articles/s41598-019-45096-0

The Slow Dog Movement

www.slowdogmovement.org

Bibliography

Forest Bathing-Nadine Mazzola

On Looking-Alexandra Horowitz

A Dog's World-Marc Bekoff, Jessica Pierce

ABOUT THE AUTHOR

Pennie Clayton works professionally with horses and dogs. She is a freelance dressage coach, advises on dog training, behaviour problems and specialises in rescue dogs, in particular sighthounds. She has lived with greyhounds and lurchers for many years and is trustee and patron for Project Galgo and advises people that adopt and foster them if they have problems settling in when they arrive from Spain.

Pennie is also a Bowen therapist and is qualified to treat humans, dogs and horses as well as writing regularly for a national magazine. She is also co-director of the Slow Dog Movement and runs scentventures for dogs at Crabtree Canine Enrichment which is in Crowborough, East Sussex

For more information and help, support, and courses on many aspects of canine wellbeing and help in keeping dogs mobile www.horseandhoundschool.co.uk

Printed in Great Britain
by Amazon